11-04

MODERN WORLD NATIONS

MODERN WORLD NATIONS

Norway

Erin Hogan Fouberg
South Dakota State University

and

Edward Patrick Hogan
South Dakota State University

Series Consulting Editor
Charles F. Gritzner
South Dakota State University

CHELSEA HOUSE
PUBLISHERS
A Haights Cross Communications Company

Frontispiece: Flag of Norway

Cover: The town of Geiranger on the shores of Geiranger Fjord.

CHELSEA HOUSE PUBLISHERS

VP, NEW PRODUCT DEVELOPMENT Sally Cheney
DIRECTOR OF PRODUCTION Kim Shinners
CREATIVE MANAGER Takeshi Takahashi
MANUFACTURING MANAGER Diann Grasse

Staff for NORWAY

EXECUTIVE EDITOR Lee Marcott
PRODUCTION EDITOR Megan Emery
PICTURE RESEARCHER 21st Century Publishing and Communications, Inc.
COVER DESIGNER Keith Trego
SERIES DESIGNER Takeshi Takahashi
LAYOUT 21st Century Publishing and Communications, Inc.

A Haights Cross Communications ⌐ Company

http://www.chelseahouse.com

First Printing

1 3 5 7 9 8 6 4 2

Library of Congress Cataloging-in-Publication Data

Fouberg, Erin Hogan.
    Norway/by Erin Hogan Fouberg and Edward Patrick Hogan.
       p. cm.—(Modern world nations)
Summary: An introduction to the geography, history, economy, government, politics,
and culture of Norway, an ancient country located at the northwestern edge of the
European continent.
    ISBN 0-7910-7479-X
    1. Norway—Juvenile literature. [1. Norway.] I. Hogan, Edward Patrick, 1939–
II. Title. III. Series.
DL409.F68 2003
948.1—dc22
                                                                                                    2003014036

Table of Contents

Norway

Tvinnefoss waterfall has dramatic views that attract Norwegians and many tourists who travel near the town of Voss in the western part of Norway.

1

Introduction to Norway

The Draugen, a terrifying sea creature that appears as a headless fisherman riding through storms in a half-boat, is one of the best-known characters in Norwegian folktales. Sighting a Draugen is considered an ominous event, signifying that death is on the horizon, usually at sea. One folktale puts a twist on the Draugen story: On one Christmas Eve, Ola encountered a Draugen, sneaked up behind him, and pushed him through a boathouse window. Ola knew the Draugen would follow him, so he ran through a churchyard full of graves, yelling, "Up, all you Christian souls, and help me!" As he fled, Ola heard the ghosts rise from their graves and battle the Draugen with coffin lids. The next morning, residents saw the remains of this fight in the scattered coffins and lids of the church graveyard. The Draugen never set foot in that area of Norway again.

The story of Ola and the Draugen parallels the story of Norway.

The country has experienced a multitude of occasions in which an outside presence has haunted its independence and its very existence. Over the course of the last millennium, for example, Denmark, Sweden, and Nazi Germany each dominated Norway for a period. Like the clever Ola, though, Norway has repeatedly drawn upon the strength of its people and their desire for independence to survive. Today, Norway is a thriving, independent country in which its people enjoy an exceptionally high standard of living.

Norway is located at the northwestern edge of the continent of Europe. Occupying part of the Scandinavian peninsula, the country is surrounded on three sides by water. On the west, Norway's rugged coastline faces the Atlantic Ocean, known at this location as the Norwegian Sea; the country's southern tip juts into the North Sea and the Skagerrak (a strait); in the north, the country faces the frigid Arctic Ocean and Barents Sea. Still farther north, the Arctic Ocean surrounds the Norwegian territory of Svalbard. The country shares land borders on its eastern side with Sweden, Finland, and Russia.

Imagine that Norway's shape resembles a southward-facing Viking ship. The greatest mass of land is in the front of the ship, with the rest of the country tapering off in a northward direction until it culminates in a dragon-like head in the northeast. In the south, its greatest width is 267 miles (420 kilometers). In the north, at its narrowest point, the country is less than 4 miles (6 kilometers) wide.

The length of Norway's continental coastline, excluding fjords, bays, and islands, is 1,647 miles (2,650 kilometers). Including fjords, bays, and thousands of offshore islands, the continental coast is 15,626 miles (25,148 kilometers) long. If the distant Norwegian territories of Svalbard and Jan Mayen are added, the coastline becomes even more extensive, at 36,122 miles (58,133 kilometers). With an area of 125,182 square miles (324,220 square kilometers), Norway is slightly larger than the state of New Mexico.

Norway is located at the northwestern edge of the continent of Europe and is surrounded on three sides by water.

The country is located roughly between 57° and 71° north latitude, and between 4° and 31° east longitude. If the islands of Svalbard are included, Norway extends slightly past 80° north latitude, and if one leaves the southern tip of Norway where it is and rotates the peninsula 180 degrees, the country would stretch as far south as Rome, Italy.

Norway's low but rugged mountains, deep valleys, active glaciers, and spectacular fjords provide some of the world's most striking scenery. It is also a "land of the midnight sun," with 24-hour periods of daylight in the summer. Beautiful sunrises and sunsets enhance summer skies. The aurora borealis ("northern lights") often dance through the dark winter sky.

Norway is also a land with an interesting history. Through the exciting early adventures of its Vikings, it dominated its neighbors, yet later, Norway became subjugated by outsiders. Today, the country is a constitutional monarchy with a government that focuses on the social welfare of its citizens, having established numerous national social, educational, health, and economic programs. All citizens are guaranteed equal access to education and health care. The government's policy of providing services in rural and urban areas alike helped delay urbanization, but today more than 70 percent of all Norwegians live in urban areas. The country has one of the highest standards of living in the world.

Christianity diffused to Norway at the end of the Viking age when, in the 1500s, the Protestant Reformation reached the country, resulting in the foundation of the Church of Norway, a part of the Evangelical Lutheran church. The state supports the church financially, and the Norwegian public schools teach the values of the church.

Norway's population now exceeds 4,500,000 citizens. Following a period of emigration during the second half of the 1800s, today Norway is experiencing immigration from Europe and many other countries. The country has also become an important economic force in today's world, not only because of its traditional strength in agriculture, fishing, forestry, and mineral extraction, but also because of its development of new industries. For example, Norway now has many sources of inexpensive power, including abundant hydroelectric power, petroleum, and natural gas. The Norwegian government controls the country's petroleum and natural gas resources and has used investment monies from these industries to help the country expand its manufacturing and to pay for its social welfare programs.

After World War II, Norway became a member of the United Nations. After the United Nations passed its Declaration on Human Rights in 1948, Norway began to change its policies toward the indigenous Sami people in the north. In the last fifty years, the country has become an important diplomatic force in international relations, hosting peace negotiations between Israel and Palestine, and more recently between the warring parties in Sri Lanka.

For centuries, from the time before the Norwegians became one of the world's most literate peoples, their sagas, folktales, and legends have been passed on from generation to generation. These oral histories are vital aspects of Norwegian culture. Sagas are generally long, ancient poems that tell the epic adventures of a warrior, chieftain, or king. Folktales normally have as their subjects royalty, animals, old women, siblings, or trolls, and while the same characters and story lines weave across folktales, many different storytellers have added their own details to the tales as they have passed them on over time. Legends, unlike folktales, generally describe facts, events, and beliefs that are part of Norwegian culture. Legends have an explanatory power, whereas folktales are for entertainment or teaching moral lessons.

We make reference to some of these sagas, folktales, and legends in introducing the chapters in this book. The stories help us see how the early Norwegians saw themselves and how they explained the world around them. Norwegians still tell and learn these stories today, and many still believe in Norwegian legends. They embrace those who came before them and the country they have constructed, thus confirming why the king's motto is "All for Norway!"

The fjords of Norway, such as the Geiranger Fjord shown here, are the most spectacular of all of Norway's glacial features. They were formed where glaciers scoured out deep U-shaped valleys.

The Physical Environment

O ne common topic of Norwegian folk legends is the country's remarkable and often breathtaking natural landscape. Early people sought to explain why the great fjords existed, why the sun shone for days during summer months, and why topographical features were formed as they were. For example, in Telemark County, by Lake Totak, rests an enormous area of scree (rock fragments). Traditionally, the people of Norway believed that the Norse god Thor created this cluster of rocks when he smashed a mountain with his fist. Such tales help geographers understand the historical relationship between the Norwegian people and their environment, even though today any physical geographer can explain that atmospheric weathering creates scree, not the violent actions of a Norse god. (Rock scree results from alternate freezing and heating of the rock surface. When water fills the cracks and voids in exposed rock and temperatures freeze, the water expands as it becomes ice and produces forces so great that rocks are split into smaller pieces and debris.)

The two principal forces involved in shaping Norway's topography (land features) are mountain building and glaciation. The Kjollen Mountains extend in a north-south direction along the western margin of the Scandinavian peninsula. This range is part of the larger Caledonian Mountains that extend beneath the North Sea and westward into Ireland. Some 600 million years ago, tectonic activity created folds and faults in the Scandinavian peninsula. Blocks of earth were uplifted and thrust over the existing landscape. Between the uplifted mountains, downfolds in the crust became the numerous basins found throughout the countryside today.

Mountains dominate Norway's physical landscape. In fact, the country's average elevation is about 1,640 feet (500 meters) above sea level and more than a quarter of the land exceeds 3,280 feet (1,000 meters) in elevation.

Glaciers are the most important erosional agent that has scoured and shaped Norway's spectacular rugged terrain. Indeed, with some 1,700 existing glaciers, the work of moving ice continues to be important even today. Ice has covered the landscape on numerous occasions over several million years. There are two types of glaciers: continental (huge ice masses covering large areas) and alpine (glaciers that form in mountains and flow into adjacent valleys). Both types have played important roles in shaping Norway's terrain. Alpine glaciers were most active on the western side of the Kjollen range, whereas continental glaciers blanketed the east.

Across a landscape, glaciers bulldoze or scrape away rock and soil from one place and deposit it in another. The enormous mass of both types of glaciers carve deeply into the land beneath. Alpine glaciers leave behind landforms such as U-shaped valleys, hanging troughs, arêtes (sharp ridges), jagged peaks, tarns

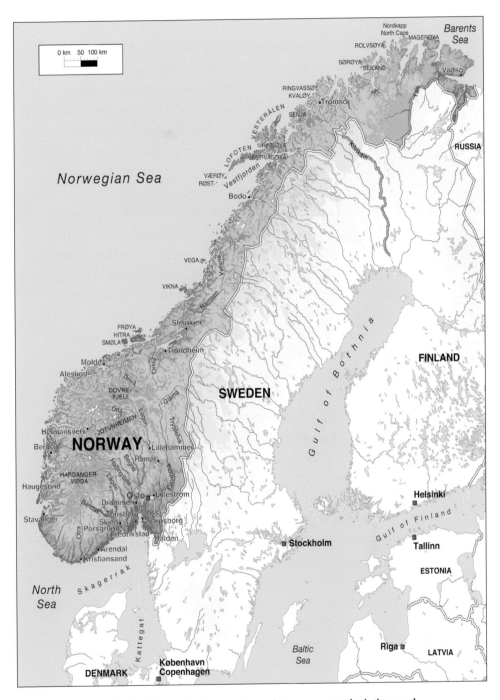

The two principal forces that have shaped Norway are glaciation and mountain building.

(mountain lakes), hanging waterfalls, and hills and ridges of debris referred to as moraine deposits. Continental glaciers leave abrasion marks in exposed bedrock, glacial lakes, rock debris deposited as stratified drift or till, and moraine (rock) deposits.

The fjords of Norway's west coast are the most spectacular of all of Norway's glacial features. Fjords were formed where glaciers scoured deep U-shaped valleys as they gouged their way to the sea. The massive glaciers carved deeply below the land surface, eroding the valleys to depths of hundreds of feet. As the glaciers melted and receded, sea levels rose and water filled the steep, rock-walled valleys today known as fjords. Smaller glacial hanging valleys and newer river valleys drain from higher elevations into the fjords, resulting in beautiful waterfalls. Arms of the sea extend deep into the Scandinavian peninsula along each fjord. Sognfjord, Hardangerfjord, and Nordfjord each extend well over 100 miles (160 kilometers) inland from the coast.

In the west, mountains and ridges shaped by glaciation reach heights of 8,000 feet (2,438 meters), dwarfing massive plateaus ranging from 4,000 to 6,000 feet (1,200 to 1,800 meters). Glacial activity continues in the region. The massive Jostedalsbreen Glacier is situated northeast of the city of Bergen and west of the Jotunheimen Mountains. This huge ice mass covers an area of roughly 310 square miles (800 square kilometers) and is the largest on the European continent.

Between Bergen and Trondheim, the Jotunheimen mountain region contains over 250 of Norway's highest peaks. Among these peaks are the impressive Galdhøpiggen, the country's tallest mountain at 8,100 feet (2,469 meters), and Glittertinden, at 8,087 feet (2,465 meters). In the southern part of the region the mountains drop off in elevation and give way to relatively flat-topped plateaus. Norwegians call such extensive areas of mountain plateaus *vidde*.

Glaciers create topographic features both as they advance and when they recede. They scour, erode (move rock debris), deposit, and form lakes. Glacial meltwater has formed an estimated 150,000 lakes, most of which are located at high elevations and in relatively isolated areas. At the end of the Ice Age, glacial meltwater caused sea level to rise worldwide. The deep, narrow, glacially scoured coastal valleys (fjords) became filled with water by the rising sea. As the sea rose, many land areas were cut off from the rest of the peninsula, leaving hundreds of islands along Norway's coast.

Continental glaciers also carved the plateaus of eastern Norway. Here, a series of mountains and plateaus drop gradually southward in elevation. In the north, elevations range from 4,800 to 3,900 feet (1,500 to 1,200 meters). Farther south, they descend to between 1,500 and 650 feet (457 and 198 meters), and eventually reach sea level on the coast.

Norway's most fertile soils and best agricultural areas are in the east. Here, too, the landscape reflects the impact of glaciers and streams as erosional agents. There are many valleys carved by both ice and water. Some valleys have beautiful, glacially scoured "finger" lakes, the name coming from their long, narrow, shape. The most notable valley is the Østerdale. Within the valley, Norway's longest river, the Glåma, flows southward into the Skagerrak. East of the valley is Norway's largest freshwater body, Lake Mjøsa.

Northern Norway is the region north of the Arctic Circle. Here, the terrain is composed mainly of high mountains and high plateaus, deeply dissected by glacial erosion. The result is a land of amazing beauty and loneliness. In places, mountains rise directly from the sea to almost 4,000 feet (1,219 meters) above sea level.

Skerryguard—a longitudinal belt of skerries, or rock formations, paralleling Norway's northern coast—protects much of the coastline. A skerry can range in size from an isolated rock to a small island. In this particular area of Norway, the guard is comprised of two rows of skerries. The outer belt is a zone of low rocks, islets, and islands dotting

Northern Norway is the region north of the Arctic Circle. This marker shows the Arctic Circle at a location in Norway.

shallow sea zones. The inner belt is formed by islands rising directly from the sea to heights of over 1,300 feet (400 meters). Both are under almost constant attack from water and wind coming off the ocean. Huge waves continually pound the skerries, tearing away any semblance of soil and scouring the remaining landscape.

Some 500 miles (800 kilometers) north of the Scandinavian peninsula is the rugged Arctic archipelago (island chain) of Svalbard. It consists of eight large islands, of which Spitsbergen is the largest, and several smaller islands and skerries. About two-thirds of Svalbard is still covered by glaciers. It is a famous geological site because its isolation and rock strata provide a relatively pristine view of geologic history.

WEATHER AND CLIMATE

Weather is the atmospheric condition of a locale at a particular moment in time. Climate is weather averaged over a long period. Atmospheric conditions are influenced by many factors. Of greatest importance are latitude, proximity to water, winds and ocean currents, and elevation.

Norway, which crosses the Arctic Circle, is located between 58° and 71° north latitude. In miles, this means that Norway actually extends some 1,100 miles (1,700 kilometers) from south to north. If Svalbard is included, Norway actually extends to the north another 750 miles (1,207 kilometers) and reaches 81° north latitude. The northern part of the Norwegian mainland and all of Svalbard lie within the Arctic region. With a range of almost 23 degrees of latitude from south to north (the United States ranges 22 degrees of latitude from southern Texas to northern North Dakota), some notable variations occur in Norway's weather and climate.

Norway's latitudes, when matched with those of North America, stretch from the Canadian city of Churchill on Hudson Bay, northward to Ellesmere Island in the Arctic Ocean. These areas of Canada are sparsely populated, yet Norway is home to 4 million people. This is largely because Norway's location on the Atlantic Ocean keeps it much warmer than comparable latitudes in the interior of North America. The earth's prevailing wind systems transport warm ocean water from the tropical latitudes to coastal northwestern Europe. It is these currents—first the Gulf Stream and then the North Atlantic Drift—that play such an important role in moderating Norway's climate.

Norway also lies in the belt of winds that blow from west to east, called the prevailing westerlies. Originating over the ocean, these moist winds carry precipitation to Norway's west coast. Although the westerlies are constant, Norway's weather is not. It can and often does change abruptly. Relatively clear, warm, pleasant days (or even hours) can suddenly turn stormy, with raging, gale-force winds, torrential rains, or blinding blizzard conditions.

Throughout the country, temperature varies greatly with terrain. As a rule of thumb, temperatures usually decrease an average of about 3.5 degrees F (1 degree C) with each 1,000-foot (305-meter) increase in elevation. Exposure to sunlight, as with a south-facing slope, also is an important factor. Locations on the leeward side of mountains (the downwind side) also tend to be warmed by descending, hence warming, winds.

Norway is home to three distinct climatic regions. The southern third of the country, extending almost to the Arctic Circle, has a temperate marine west coast climate. The westerlies blowing onshore moderate the four seasons. Both winters and summers are milder than their more continental counterparts. Significant variations in precipitation amounts occur in the mountains and plateaus based on location and elevation. Precipitation is well distributed, but there is a notable variation from winter to summer. Winter is the wettest season and summer is the driest, because as the subtropical high over the Atlantic Ocean moves northward, it brings with it increased aridity, which results in a decrease in summer rains. As the westerlies reach Norway, the moist air rises over the mountains, releasing precipitation as it cools at higher elevations. The heavier precipitation, then, falls on the western side of the mountains. Having released its moisture, air flows down the eastern side of the mountains, creating a drier climate, especially in the summer.

Most of the northern two-thirds of Norway and all of Svalbard have a polar (or tundra) climate. This frigid climate also occurs in the northern fringes of North America, Europe, and Asia. It is characterized by very long, cold winters and short summers. Norwegian winters are not as severe as might be expected because the North Atlantic and Arctic Oceans exert a moderating influence on the land. Nevertheless, because of the high latitudes, the sun is always low above the horizon and, indeed, disappears for lengthy periods (days to months, depending upon latitude) in winter. Annual precipitation is light here, with the heaviest amounts falling during the brief summer months.

A small coastal area in the northwest, extending from Bodø to Lofoten, has a humid continental climate. This small area is actually at the extreme western edge of a climatic zone that extends eastward across much of north central Eurasia. Although found in only a small part of Norway, this climate zone covers extensive areas of neighboring Sweden and Finland. The humid continental climate is one of extremes. Precipitation ranges from very light to moderate in the short summer, to moderate snowfall in the long winter season. Snow covers the land much of the year, and temperature variation by season is greater than in the rest of Norway.

No matter where one lives in Norway, the climate has four seasons. The duration and intensity of these seasons vary significantly by location. In the south and along the southern coastal areas, the average temperatures generally range from 0° F (−17.7° C) in the winter to 77° F (25° C) in the summer. In the north, temperature extremes can range from−62° F (−52° C) in the winter to 86° F (30° C) in the summer. The record low in Norway occurred in the interior at Finnmark, where the temperature dropped to−60.5° F (−51.4° C).

THE MIDNIGHT SUN

Because of its geographic position, Norway is often referred to as "the Land of the Midnight Sun." Locations north of the Arctic Circle, including northern Norway and Svalbard, receive 24 hours of sunlight around the time of the summer solstice, June 21. Similarly, around the winter solstice, December 21, these locations lie in 24-hour darkness. At Tromsø, located at about 69° north latitude, the sun does not appear above the horizon at all between November 27 and January 15. Conversely, complete daylight extends from May 20 through July 22, a period when the sun never sets below the horizon.

SOILS

Six factors influence soil formation: terrain, parent materials, time, vegetation, biological activity, and climate. Because these factors vary in intensity and importance from place to place, Norway's soils also are varied. Most are classified as "mountain soils," characterized by infertility. Because of its climate and soils only a few small areas of Norway support crop production.

FLORA

In Norway, as elsewhere, climate is a primary influence on the flora (natural vegetation). Since climate varies with elevation, Norway's flora varies across the country's mountains and plateaus. Norway spruce (blue spruce) and pine trees cover the lower mountain sides. Spruce is most dominant in the southeast and midlands. As the elevation increases, deciduous trees such as birch, aspen, and mountain ash replace the conifers. Higher up still are sparse areas of low-growing birch and willow trees hugging the ground for protection, gradually giving way to tundra, bare rock, and ice. Other deciduous species such as oak, elm, and maple scatter the south shoreline and areas of central Norway.

Other plant life varies greatly by climate and location. Among the most notable are the purple heather and star hyacinth found in temperate western coastal areas, foxglove and holly in the southwest, and aconite and blue anemone in the east. In the tundra and other mountain zones, mosses and lichens cover the landscape, with wildflowers scattered throughout.

Norway also has plant life that is not native to the Scandinavian peninsula. One can find species that originated in England, Central Europe, Siberia, Asia, and even North America. Tracing the diffusion routes of these species is fascinating detective work for the biologists who are trying to learn when, why, and how these plants came to Norway. Numerous theories abound—including birds, wind, and water as the agents of diffusion—but little consensus or conclusive evidence exists.

FAUNA

With the end of the Ice Age and the opening of newly exposed lands, fauna (animal life) began moving into the Scandinavian peninsula. Among the early arrivals were wild reindeer, accompanied by predators such as bear, wolf, wolverine, and arctic fox. Large numbers of elk, deer, wild boar, marten, fox, beaver, otter, squirrel, and hare later followed them. The herds of reindeer and elk were especially important, because they provided food for the predators. Wild boar disappeared from the hostile environment after only a short time. Over time, some species of Norwegian animals and birds developed camouflaging coloring either to protect themselves or to improve their hunting success.

Today between 15,000 and 20,000 wild reindeer still survive in Norway. Far more numerous are the domesticated reindeer herds of the north, which outnumber the wild by a factor of at least ten. Polar bears can still be found on the Svalbard archipelago. Other predators, such as the wolf, wolverine, and

These are among the many domesticated reindeer that live in Norway. Hundreds of reindeer scramble onto Kvaloya Island after swimming from the coast of Norway's arctic Finnmark province in the spring. Sami herders drive their reindeer from the inland tundra to the lush coast.

lynx, that once roamed Norway are now gone. Without these predators, elk herds are growing significantly.

Other animal species include a variety of rats and small rodents. The most notable rodent is the furry little lemming. Lemmings are up to 6 inches (15 centimeters) long. Every 11 or 12 years they experience an enormous population increase that generally ends with millions of lemmings falling over cliffs, drowning in the sea, or being eaten by predators as they migrate. These migration periods are known as lemming years. During that time other animals and birds thrive by feeding on young and feeble lemmings. Birds such as the grouse and snowy owl do especially well during these times. Remarkably, during lemming years the snowy owl somehow knows that it is time to travel thousands of miles across the Eurasian tundra to Norway to feast on the small rodents.

Norway is also home to a wide variety of birds, including the raven, eagle, gyrfalcon, wood grouse, black grouse, partridge, owl, woodpecker, crane, whooper swan, grebe, goose, and duck. Millions of cliff nesters occupy the coastal areas, including cormorants, gulls, and the colorful puffin. Norway was once home to the flightless and now extinct great auk. Today, the sea eagle, the most spectacular of all Norway's birds, is on the endangered species list. The government is making major efforts to restore the sea eagle population.

Sea life comprises a major part of Norway's fauna. The coastal areas are home to a great variety of sea life ranging from whales and seals to such fish species as cod, halibut, and haddock. There are also shrimp and a variety of other shellfish. Norway's rivers are home to such fish as river salmon, trout, perch, and pike.

Two other animals that deserve attention are the Norwegian fjord horse and the Norwegian elkhound. While both animals are bred and domesticated, both are also unique to Norway. The small fjord horse is one of the oldest horse breeds in the world, purportedly over 4,000 years old. The Norwegian

There are millions of cliff-nesting birds in Norway including these colonies of Brunnich's Guillemots and Black-Legged Kittiwakes.

elkhound is a small- to medium-sized hunting dog. Elkhounds look like small Alaskan huskies.

WATER

It is difficult to think of Norway without picturing in one's mind the deep, dark blue waters of the country's west coast fjords and the spectacular interlaced waterfalls cascading down the steep adjacent valley walls. Norway is indeed a land of water. It is found frozen in glaciers and impounded in lakes and reservoirs. It flows rapidly downstream in rivers and waterfalls. The ground is saturated with water, and seawater surrounds much of the country, lapping at its shores and filling its spectacular fjords.

Glaciers contain vast supplies of fresh water frozen thousands of years ago. Like giant ice cubes upon the landscape, glaciers eventually enter zones where weather and climatic factors enable the water to escape from its solid state and become a free-flowing liquid. This glacial meltwater is a primary source of moisture for Norway's many rivers, lakes, and wetlands. Indeed, some people claim that Norway contains over 250,000 rivers, streamlets, lakes, and ponds. Because of the mountainous terrain and coastal location, numerous short, cascading, quite cold, and shallow rivers start and end in Norway. The many streams provide the country with excellent potential for hydropower development. Additionally, some 400 to 500 of these streams are noted for their salmon fishing and are therefore important for tourism. Many streams drain into fjords, whereas others flow into lakes and ponds.

Norway's principal river is the Glåma, which drains from Lake Aursunden, located southeast of Trondheim, southward to Fredrikstad on the Oslofjorden. It is approximately 372 miles (611 kilometers) long. The Glåma and the Lågen River, which runs parallel to the west, form a combined river basin that is one of the world's greatest hydroelectric power-producing regions. Lake Mjøsa, a reservoir on the Lågen, is Norway's largest freshwater body.

Norway's lakes and rivers are experiencing serious problems as a result of acid rain, which is rainfall that contains increased acidity due to atmospheric pollution. Wetlands have dried out, fish kills have occurred, and lime is even being added to streams to clean the water. The acid rain stems from several sources, including the burning of fossil fuels, petroleum leaks, use of fertilizers, polluted water runoff, and salty rains from the sea. Norway has actively addressed this environmental challenge by enacting a variety of laws to prevent further pollution and to protect its waters, water rights, hydropower, industry, wildlife, and fishing.

MINERALS

Nonmetallic minerals of importance in Norway include industrial minerals, dimension stones, and construction minerals. Nonmetallic minerals are those which are primarily quarried rather than mined. Industrial minerals consist of limestone and dolomite for cement, lime, and filler; olivine for iron and steel smelting; and syenite for glass and ceramics. Dimension stones include granite, gneiss, marble, flagstone, and slate for buildings, monuments, and related outdoor uses. Construction minerals consist of crushed rock, sand and gravel, and clays, and are used in building the country's transportation and building infrastructure.

Norway's metallic (mined) minerals include iron ore, copper, zinc, lead, gold, nickel, and ilmenite. Until twenty years ago, iron ore was Norway's most important mineral, but production has declined significantly, and while gold, silver, copper, lead, and zinc can be found in Norway, none of them is being mined commercially today. There is still some nickel production. Ilmenite, which is used in paint, plastic, and paper production, is the most important metallic mineral in Norway today, but even that is of minor importance when compared to the economic contribution of the country's mineral fuels and nonmetallic minerals.

The most important of Norway's minerals is its mineral fuels, including petroleum, natural gas, and coal. Combined, the production of oil and natural gas exceeds $25 billion a year (172 billion Norwegian Krone). This amounts to over 23 percent of the Norwegian gross domestic product (GDP). Oil and gas production is concentrated in the North Sea and on Norway's continental shelf, an underwater area extending into the Norwegian Sea that is four times larger than the country's landmass itself. The primary production area is known as the Ekofisk district. The petroleum and natural gas are moved to refineries and markets by pipelines or tankers. Norway provides about 20 percent of Western Europe's natural gas needs.

Coal production is concentrated at Svalbard, where a second major mine was opened recently. Svalbard coal is of high quality and well suited to industrial use. It is shipped to the Norwegian mainland where it is used primarily for industry and power production.

This sod-roofed dwelling in Stavanger is a preserved remnant of Stone-Age Norway.

3

Culture History

Norwegians used stories not only to explain their physical landscape, but to also explain the horrible catastrophes and other major events that brought change to their cultural landscape. In 1349, for example, the black plague moved into Norway from the European continent. The effects were immediate as the disease ravaged villages, towns, and rural settlements. Some places lost nearly their entire population, yet others were relatively untouched by the deadly disease. Norwegians used a folk legend to explain and describe the patterns of death resulting from the black plague. According to this legend, death came in the form of an old woman with a rake and a broom. When she raked the landscape, some people lived. Where she used her broom, death followed as she swept everyone from the landscape. In isolated areas and in extreme environments, the old woman used her rake, and a smaller proportion of the population died. In urban areas, such as Oslo, Trondheim, and Bergen, the old woman used her broom, and these areas suffered terrible losses. Norway as a whole lost about 350,000 people to the black plague, about half its population at the time.

This chapter focuses on major events affecting Norway's cultural landscape, offering explanations more realistic than rakes and brooms! A cultural landscape is the visible imprint of human activities on Earth's surface. Examples of cultural landscape features include: buildings; transportation arteries; the rerouting of rivers, building of dams, and creation of reservoirs; and the way rural lands are divided into farms. Present cultural landscapes also can provide clues to earlier human activities and resulting landscapes.

EARLIEST OCCUPANTS

Some 12,000 years ago, the great glaciers that for eons had covered vast areas of Eurasia and North America retreated. In Norway, the newly emerged landscape was rugged, rock-strewn, mountainous, and still covered in many areas by lingering pockets of ice. The weather was harsh and posed constant challenges to life. Evidence indicates, however, that as the climate warmed and the land began to blossom with plants, it was quickly occupied by various forms of animal life. Humans soon followed.

Following the Ice Age, Stone-Age human occupants appear to have first arrived in Norway from present-day Central Asia. There is some indication that they were the ancestors of the Sami (formerly called "Lapps"), who now occupy northern Norway. They lived at a subsistence level, in small territorial bands, hunting moose, reindeer, and seal, and fishing for salmon. Like traditional folk cultures elsewhere, they used virtually every part of their fish and animal catch, and also learned to use the beneficial properties of the plant life found in their local environ-ment. They migrated across the region seasonally, carrying their possessions with them. Little evidence of their existence remains except for some stone tools, cairns (stone piles or monuments), and petroglyphs (rock carvings). Rock carvings at Alta Fjord, in far northern Norway, provide the most significant evidence of their early existence. This site contains thousands of paintings and carvings and has been designated a World Heritage Site.

ARRIVAL OF GERMANIC PEOPLE

Eventually, Germanic people began moving into Norway. They first moved northward along the coast from Denmark, staying relatively close to the shore. They lived by fishing and collecting coastal marine life. Evidence indicates that they moved as far north as Trondheim. A study of the cultural landscape shows they were concentrated in southern Norway. This is known from the spatial distribution of middens (trash heaps) and shells they left behind. Virtually every human society (and many animals, as well) leave middens. These refuse piles enable archaeologists, biologists, geographers, and others to study human settlement, movements, artifacts, diets, and many other aspects of a people's culture.

ARRIVAL OF AGRICULTURE AND ITS IMPACT

Evidence indicates that, about 5,000 years ago, agricultural practices were introduced into the Oslofjord area in southern Norway as a result of contact with neighbors to the south. Agriculture appears to have arrived in southern Sweden and Denmark about the same time. Most likely the occupants of these areas learned about crop and livestock practices and obtained Stone-Age tools and implements from neighboring societies and through trade with other European peoples. With the arrival of agriculture, people now had new ways to gain a livelihood in Norway. Ironically, evidence shows that at about the same time Europe introduced agricultural practices to Norway, the climate of the Scandinavian peninsula cooled. While that may have slowed the country's transition to an agricultural society, it certainly did not stop it.

Beginning in about 1800 B.C. and lasting until 500 B.C., the Bronze Age changed life in southern Norway. Agricultural settlements increased in number. Bronze Age tools and weapons also arrived in the region through trade with people to the south. In the far north, people still relied on hunting and fishing for their livelihood. Rock carvings, stone pillars, stone cairns, earthen burial mounds, and solar wheels indicate that the people were likely sun worshipers. The island of Karmøy northwest of Stavanger has the best examples of these cultural landscapes. Near the town of Kopervik are numerous examples of Bronze Age stone pillars and burial mounds. In fact, archaeologists have not yet excavated the largest such mound, Doa Hill. Rock carvings include symbolic cuplike depressions, ships, animals, fish, and weapons. Bronze Age tools and weapons found through excavations are on display in municipal and national museums.

DAWN OF THE IRON AGE

In about 500 B.C., the Iron Age reached Norway. This period lasted almost a thousand years. Iron tools, implements, and weapons came into the area from the Germanic south. A variety of evidence, including tools, glass, and Latin lettering, indicates contact also occurred with the Roman world. Roman and Greek maps from the time often included an island north of Denmark, Thule. Relative knowledge of Norway existed, but knowledge of the absolute location, size, and shape of Norway and Sweden was lacking.

Knowledge and use of bronze and iron instruments extended both inland and along the coast to north of the Arctic Circle. During this period, the first runic inscriptions (based on an early Germanic alphabet) began appearing on freestanding rocks, stones, and gravestones. Symbols found in early rock carvings are believed to have been both literate and mystical. The runic alphabet was likely developed around 200 B.C., most likely in Sweden. It has ties to both the

Roman italic alphabet and the earlier Greek alphabet. The runic alphabet became the alphabet of the Scandinavian and Northern Germanic peoples.

Despite ongoing contact with the people of the outside world, Norwegians existed in tremendous isolation. They lived primarily in extended family groups, often defined by the valley or fjord they occupied and their way of obtaining a livelihood. This way of life resulted in the development of numerous petty kingdoms, each ruled by a chieftain. Several petty kingdoms could meet together and form an even larger kingdom. Such merging continued until these petty kingdoms appear to have formed alliances ultimately resulting in only four larger kingdoms.

VIKING ERA

By the eighth century, European people began referring to the Norwegians (which means "people of the north") as the Vikings to designate them as people who came from the fjords. The word *vikr* means fjord or inlet; a *vik* is the area of fertile soil at the farthest point (the curve) of a fjord. The Viking Age began for the Norwegians in about 793 A.D. when Vikings attacked England and plundered the English monastery on the North Sea island of Lindisfarne. Viking peoples also occupied the Orkney, Shetland, and Hebrides islands and the Isle of Man.

Over the next three centuries, Vikings dominated much of Europe. They gained control over most of England and Ireland and occupied extensive areas of both islands. They sailed the rivers of central Europe and Russia and occupied portions of western Russia (the name "Russia" itself is of Viking origin). Viking ships entered the Mediterranean Sea to the south and sailed west to Iceland and Greenland. There is strong evidence that, under Leif Eriksson, they reached the coast of North America in 1001.

The Vikings plundered the monasteries, farmlands, and

This Viking ship has been dated to the ninth century A.D. and is now displayed in the Viking Ship Museum in Oslo. Such ships sailed the rivers of Europe, the Mediterranean Sea, and sailed west to Iceland and Greenland. Leif Eriksson is believed to have reached the coast of North America in such a ship in about 1000 A.D.

cities in their path. They also introduced urban life to the Irish with the establishment of urban forts and trading communities at Dublin, Galway, and other cities. Viking raiding parties first arrived in Ireland in 820 A.D. Monasteries there built the famous round towers that dot the Irish countryside as treasure houses designed to be safe from Viking attack. These efforts did little to slow the Vikings, however, as the fierce warriors took what they wanted, including people, who were kept or traded as slaves.

Harald the Fair-Haired conquered many of the petty kings in the Oslofjord region and unified much of Norway under his rule. In 874, some people escaping Harald's rule sailed past Ireland to Iceland, another island but one with an environment similar to that of Norway, and became the island's first inhabitants. Civilization thrived on Iceland, and by 930, it established itself as the Icelandic Commonwealth. Unfortunately for emigrating Vikings, however, arable land was as rare in Iceland as at home. As a result, it was not long before they had to move even further west to Greenland and eventually to North America.

In 995, Olav Tryggvessøn, one of Harald the Fair-Haired's great-grandsons, arrived in Norway from England to assume the throne of Norway (as Olav I). Olav was a Viking who had been raised in England and had converted to Christianity. He built a new capital at Trondheim and set out to establish Christianity as the religion of the land. The pagan Vikings had successfully fought off earlier attempts to Christianize them. The Vikings joined with Danes and Swedes to defeat Olav's forces in a naval battle. Realizing defeat, Olav jumped overboard, choosing to drown rather than surrender. His actions made him a hero to Norwegians then and now.

Shortly after Olav Tryggvessøn 's death in 1000, his future successor, Olav Haraldson (Olav II), began a naval career in England. Olav II became king of Norway in 1016. His famous career included destruction of the London Bridge on the Thames River in England. When the Danish king Canute invaded Norway in 1028, he interrupted Olav II's efforts to lead Norway. Olav II fled to Kiev, only to return when he thought the time was right. However, he was killed upon his arrival as a result of an ongoing dispute between members of his kingdom and the family of Erling Skjalgson from Jren. Norwegians considered Olav II a martyr for Christianity, and he was subsequently elevated to sainthood within the Roman Catholic Church. Even today, Saint Olav remains the patron saint of Norway. The well of Saint Olav is in Karmy, and pilgrims believe its waters have healing powers.

A woman of Irish royalty is also listed among those who first brought Christianity to Norway. Saint Sunniva and her followers fled an invading pagan king by moving to a cave on the Norwegian island of Selje. A landslide sealed off the cave, killing Saint Sunniva and others. In about 995, people began seeing unusual lights on Selje. King Olav I sent people to the island to investigate. They opened the cave and found Saint Sunniva's perfectly preserved body. Olav I then built a church there to honor her faith. The remains of a Benedictine cloister on Selje, dedicated to Saint Sunniva, can still be visited by tourists and pilgrims.

In 1038, following an unsuccessful treaty with Denmark, Harald Hardåde became king of Norway. He established the city of Oslo, which is now the country's capital. He also attempted to conquer England, which was then ruled by his cousin, King Harold. When Harald Hardåde died in the Battle of Stamford Bridge, Viking efforts to conquer England also ended.

During the Viking Age, Norwegian rule dominated a far larger geographic area than the Norway of today. The Viking kingdom of Norway at one time or another was comprised of present-day Norway, a span of northern Europe that stretched from the British Isles eastward to Russia, and Iceland, Greenland, and for a short period even Newfoundland. While not as extensive or as wealthy as Rome, Viking Norway was a formidable military empire.

Evidence of the Viking culture still appears on Norway's cultural landscape. One of the most significant examples is at Borre Nasjonalpark west of the Oslofjorden. Borre is Norway's oldest national park and is the resting place of Viking kings, who are buried in very large, grass-covered earthen mounds.

Other evidence of the Viking culture includes the ships, weaponry, and other artifacts found in the Vikingskipshuset (Viking Ship Museum) in Oslo. The remains of a Viking fortress and tower can be seen in Tonsberg. Viking artifacts in the form of weapons, tools, jewelry, woodcarving, and runic stones can be found in many locations. Similarly, Viking sagas, folktales, games, and gods still play important roles in Norwegian life.

Harald was succeeded by his sons Magnus II and Olav the Peaceful. Olav the Peaceful is most noted for founding the cities of Bergen and Stavanger. As Harald's sons and their successors, including Sigurd I, died off, Norway reached a point, in 1130, when no direct royal descendants of Harald the Fair-Haired remained. This began a long period during which Norway found itself devoid of true leadership. No strong king or kings ruled the land. Instead, merchants from the Hanseatic League (a trading association) and the leaders of the newly established bishoprics of the Roman Catholic Church became the power brokers of Norway.

With the ascension of King Haakon IV in 1217, the power of the monarchy began to return to Norway. His grandson Haakon V made Oslo the country's capital. Haakon V feared invasion by Sweden and reasoned that by moving the capital to the east and interior, it strengthened the defense of Norway. Over time, as Viking control overseas waned, Norwegian royalty began to emerge as a force of stability within the country, and Christianity increased in importance.

Around this time, another fascinating feature began to appear on the cultural landscape in the form of the stave kirk (church). Norwegians built the first stave churches about one thousand years ago. These churches, built out of narrow vertical strips of wood, are fascinating features of the landscape because they reflect the physical environment in which they were built, particularly the readily available supply of wood. The above-ground sills reflect the need to preserve the wood from below-ground weathering. The kirks also reflect the culture of the builders, incorporating features, tools, and techniques used by Norwegian shipbuilders and ornate wood-carvings dating back to the Viking Age.

The stave church provides Norwegian Christians a unique house in which to worship their God. Although as many as 1,200 such churches existed, today only 29 remain in Norway. They are preserved in such communites as Song, Telemark, Oslo, Trondheim, and Oppland. Several have been rebuilt, some have been relocated to museums and cultural parks, and others are deteriorating and in need of restoration. People of Norwegian descent have built replicas in several other areas around the world, such as Rapid City, South Dakota.

OUTSIDE RULE

Historically, the nature of Norway's royalty has been complex and not easily understood. Throughout much of its history, Norway was ruled by outside powers. Viking kings reigned until 1380, when King Olav VI became the ruler of both Denmark and Norway. Royal rule followed his lineage until 1814, when Carl XIII, king of Sweden, gained control of the land. Finally, in 1905, after centuries of outside domination, Haakon VII became the king of Norway. Intermarriage among the ruling families of Denmark, Norway, and Sweden helped contribute to this foreign influence. In the late 1300s, for example, Queen Margrethe, a Dane, married King Haakon VI of Norway (a son of the king of Sweden). Following the death of Haakon VI in 1387, Queen Margrethe became ruler of the land. She led Norway into a union with Denmark and Sweden, which was signed at Kalmar, Sweden, on Trinity Sunday 1397.

As a result of the Union of Kalmar, Denmark and Norway became one. Sweden never really became absorbed into the union, choosing instead to participate with the union when it was to its advantage to do so and to oppose it when it needed to protect its independence. Norway under Margrethe and her

This stave church in Oslo is one of the oldest churches in the country. These churches were built with narrow strips of wood and are a reflection of the ready availability of wood.

successors essentially became a province dominated by Danish royalty and merchants. This domination lasted until 1814. During this time, the Danish language became the official language of Norway. A Danish king with a local governor ruled the country, and Danish merchants controlled all trade, retaining the profits for themselves.

In 1534, Christian III became king of Denmark and Norway, following an unsuccessful attempt by some to prevent him from assuming the crown because he was a Lutheran. In 1536, he made Lutheranism the religion of Denmark and imposed it on Norway (which he called the Dependency of Denmark). Christian III abolished Catholic dioceses and churches, replaced the Catholic clergy with Protestant Danes, and even replaced the Latin Bible with a Danish-language translation.

In the seventeenth century, many rural Norwegian people embraced Pietism, a belief system that focused on ethics, purity, personal devotion, charity, and mysticism rather than on Catholic-based teachings and traditions. By mixing Pietism with Protestant theology, Norway's Evangelical Lutheran church emerged. It enforced Lutheran creed with zeal. Strict rules and policies were imposed on all society, and the church sought to make membership universal throughout Norway.

Mandatory Lutheranism also affected the stave churches, especially in rural areas. Congregations added on to the buildings as their numbers grew. Remodeling included lowering the ceilings, adding windows, and painting over ecclesiastical art. Over the centuries, new churches were built using wood, building stone, and other basic materials. Other than a few large churches, such as the cathedral at Trondheim, and some more recent and modern buildings, most of Norway's churches are architecturally simple and functional.

Norway's union with Denmark ended in 1814. Denmark had allied itself with France during the Napoleonic Wars. At this time, Norwegians experienced widespread famine since they were isolated from the trade they normally depended on with other regions of Europe. With the defeat of France, Sweden (a victor in the wars) claimed Norway.

Political forces in Norway saw this as an opportunity to reestablish royalty and enact a new constitution. Assembling in Eidsvoll, Norwegians created and—on May 17, 1814—adopted their own constitution and chose Christian Fredrick as king. (May 17 is celebrated annually as the Syttende Mai, or Constitution Day.) The assembly's actions spurred open conflict between Sweden and Norway. The armies of King Carl Johan of Sweden dominated, however, and, following negotiations, King Christian Fredrick's rule ended on November 4, 1814.

Beginning around 1825, famine, hunger, warfare, and

poverty in Norway encouraged people to seek a better life in North America. This was the start of a long period of migration from the rural areas of Norway to the richer agricultural areas of the American Midwest. Today, the descendants of the emigrants comprise large portions of the populations of Minnesota, Wisconsin, Illinois, Iowa, South Dakota, and North Dakota. Between 1825 and today, over 900,000 people moved from Norway to the United States.

The reasons for migration were many, but among the major factors were: the American Homestead Act, which opened lands in the Midwest to settlers; political freedoms, including the right to vote; higher wages; urban life; and over-population in rural Norway. One of the benefits to Norway of this out-migration to America was less pressure to split up family farms in rural Norway. This enabled some Norwegian families to retain, and eventually to expand, their landholdings in their homeland.

During the period of Swedish rule, the Storting (Norwegian Parliament) functioned, but with little power. In 1905, the Storting voted to establish separate Norwegian embassies and offices around the world. The king of Sweden responded that Norway was part of Sweden, not an independent country. The Storting then conducted a national referendum on August 13, 1905, to see if the people of Norway wanted to become independent or remain with Sweden. The vote was 368,208 for independence and a mere 184 for remaining with Sweden. Sweden gave up, and the Kingdom of Norway was reborn.

INDEPENDENCE AND TROUBLED TIMES

After gaining independence in 1905, Norway's Storting sought to build a strong foundation for an independent Norway. One of its first acts was to invite Danish prince Carl to become King Haakon VII of Norway. King Haakon VII ruled from 1905 to 1957. Although he was often referred to as the Happy King because of his impressive smile, he also was a man of action.

He was responsible for keeping Norway neutral during World War I and stood up to Nazi demands during World War II, refusing to abdicate the throne.

Also shortly after independence, World War I began. Norway declared its neutrality, but Norwegian shipping and trade suffered great losses at home and on the sea. Because Norway relies so heavily on imported food, this loss of trade created serious problems for some time. One of the most disastrous outcomes of the depressed economic times between the two World Wars, and particularly the Great Depression beginning in 1929, was the emergence of Adolf Hitler and the Nazi Party in Germany. A decade later, in 1939, Germany invaded Poland and World War II began. In a short period of time, Germany occupied Poland, Austria, France, the Benelux countries (Belgium, the Netherlands, and Luxembourg), Yugoslavia, Denmark, and Norway. Norway had again declared neutrality, but German forces invaded by sea and air on April 9, 1940.

Before the German invasion, the Storting had passed a resolution stating that in case of occupation, the government could continue to operate in exile. Government leaders and members of the Norwegian royal family escaped Nazi capture on a British naval ship. The royal family resided in exile in Britain during the war and continued to function as Norway's official government. Meanwhile, in Norway, Vidkun Quisling, a Nazi sympathizer, claimed the power to form a new Norwegian government loyal to Germany. During the war, thousands of Norwegians fled for Sweden. Others were taken into concentration camps and killed by the Nazis. Many other Norwegians perished because of the food shortages in the country.

The Norwegian people resisted Hitler and Quisling's program as best they could. This included work slowdowns, reduced fish catches, flight to avoid conscription into the German army, and attacks on installations and German troops. Perhaps the most important act of the Norwegian resistance

Even though Norway declared its neutrality in World War II, German troops invaded by sea and air in 1940. These German troops made landfall on the Norway coast.

effort was the sabotage of the Norsk Hydroplant at Telemark. Because of that act, the Nazis were prevented access to heavy water, essential for manufacturing atomic bombs.

MODERN NORWAY

In 1945, King Haakon VII returned to Norway from exile in Britain. Norway, seeking to play a role in efforts to establish world peace, joined the United Nations in 1945 and the North Atlantic Treaty Organization (NATO) in 1949. It also sought to establish economic and political protections by joining the Nordic Council with Denmark, Sweden, Finland, and Iceland in 1952.

Surprisingly, despite an invitation to join the European Union (EU) in 1973 and again in 1994, a small majority of the Norwegian people voted against membership. This was a significant and far-reaching decision. Norway is one of only a handful of European countries that remains independent, but the question arises—at what price? With membership comes many important economic, social, and political benefits. The EU's move to a single monetary system based on the Euro has substantially affected tourism and trade. In 1992, an agreement on the European Economic Area (EEA) between the EU and the European Free Trade Association (EFTA) gave Norway ongoing participation in the EEA. Despite that agreement and the deeply entrenched split over the EU among the Norwegian people, the real question is whether Norway will be able to continue resisting EU membership. The answer to that question is something the rest of Europe, and the world, will watch closely.

In 1994, the Olympic Winter Games were held at Lillehammer, Norway. This event was a time of great celebration for the people of Norway. The Olympics provided an opportunity to show the entire world how far the country has come in a hundred years of independence. It also gave the world a glimpse of Norway's beautiful countryside and wonderful people.

In summary, since the decline of Viking influences, except for brief periods of independence, Norway has been dominated, exploited, and occasionally even overlooked by more powerful neighbors. Foreign powers exploited Norway's natural resources and controlled trade. They imposed not only a new religion but a state religion. They kept the Norwegian people at a low standard of living. Nearly a million people left the country in search of better opportunities and freedom elsewhere.

With true independence and the recent discovery of extensive petroleum and natural gas deposits, Norway is now in a new position. Its unique forms of social welfare intertwined with capitalism have allowed the country to achieve one of the world's highest standards of living. Norway has also developed plans to protect the economic and social well-being of its people in the future. The result is a contemporary country that integrates the history, traditions, and artifacts of the past with contemporary technologies and economies to produce a truly unique Norwegian cultural landscape.

Beginning in the early nineteenth century many Norwegians sought a better life in North America. This trend continued into the twentieth century with many leaving on ships such as this S.S. *Angelo*, shown leaving the port of Christiane, Norway in 1905.

CHAPTER

4

People and Culture

In Norse mythology, the mountains south of Trondheim and north of Bergen, the Jotunheimen, were known as the home of the bad giants. In fact, the word "jotun" means giant. This toponym (place name) certainly discouraged Norwegian settlement in the area for centuries. Today, the area is embraced as one of the most remarkable landscapes in Norway. It is home to the country's two tallest mountain peaks as well as to dozens of peaks taller than 6,500 feet (2,000 meters). Norwegians and foreign tourists visit the Jotunheimen on vacation, but few Norwegians live in these mountains, or in the glaciated area to the west, the Breheimen.

POPULATION SETTLEMENT AND DENSITY

Norway's population distribution and density corresponds closely to the country's climate and terrain. Very few people live in the cold, rugged mountainous regions and the far north, resulting in a density of fewer than 2 persons per square mile (1 per square kilometer). Most of the country has a density ranging from 3 to 15 people per square mile (2–8 per square kilometer). The country's greatest population densities occur in and around the capital and largest city, Oslo. Oslo County has nearly 2,000 people per square mile (1,200 people per square kilometer). Areas adjacent to the capital, including Akershus and Vestfold counties, have densities exceeding 100 per square mile (60 per square kilometer). The population of these three counties, plus Ostfold, another county in the greater Oslo region, is nearly 1.5 million, or roughly 32 percent of Norway's 4,525,000 people.

What is perhaps most remarkable about Norway's distribution of population and settlement is its relatively equal distribution across most of the country's habitable counties. The people of Norway historically have lived in scattered settlements and small rural villages as well as in large cities such as Oslo and Bergen. Of Norway's 19 counties, only one, Finnmark, has a population below 100,000 people. As might be expected, Finnmark occupies the country's entire northern tip. The most populated counties are Oslo (composed of the city of Oslo), Akershus (adjacent to Oslo), and Hordaland (including the city of Bergen), each with population over 400,000. The urbanization movement in Norway came relatively late, during the latter half of the nineteenth century. Today, about 75 percent of the population, however, lives in urban areas.

The fertility rate of most European countries has fallen below replacement level (2.1 births per woman). With fewer children being born, the population of Europe is rapidly aging. Norway's neighbor, Sweden, has one of the lowest fertility rates in Europe, 1.57 percent. Norway's late urbanization and policy of supporting populations in rural areas have helped keep its fertility rate higher, at 1.85, although still well below replacement level. Even so, the country's population is growing at a rate of roughly .5 percent per year. Growth is the result of immigration, however, rather than births in excess of deaths.

HEALTH CARE AND SOCIAL SERVICES

Quality of health care is an important benchmark of the success of a government's welfare program. Norway guarantees universal and equal access to medical care for all its people, regardless of geographic location, income, employment status, or age. Health care normally begins with a local doctor. Numerous community hospitals serve local needs and facilitate movement of patients to more specialized treatment centers if needed. While taxes are collected at the state level, the local governments are responsible for budgeting and allocating health-care funds. Each of the nineteen counties has at least one hospital. Despite this level of accessibility, the jagged, fjorded coastland and inhabited islands of the west cause many rural areas to still be a ferry ride away from a hospital or other more specialized medical care.

Often, health-care benefits overlap with social services. This policy creates a strong network of support for Norway's aging population. Norwegians generally agree the elderly should continue to live in their own homes as long as possible rather than moving into retirement centers or nursing homes. Through its social service programs, the country provides at-home nursing care for its elderly. These services include helping the elderly obtain mobility equipment (such as wheelchairs), helping them bathe, delivering meals, and even providing housekeeping services.

Because the state provides a basic pension to retired citizens, including those who were never employed, very few elderly in Norway live below the poverty line (only about 5 percent). Elderly Norwegians who are retired from a job earn pensions based on the salary they earned when working.

SAFETY AND SECURITY

The safety of the population is the responsibility of the police force. In some areas it is supplemented by the Night Ravens (citizen's patrol). Crime rates in Norway are low compared to those of other European countries or the United States. People are generally safe walking the streets of the larger cities late at night. There are exceptions in some parts of the larger urban centers, where alcohol and drugs are problems.

EMIGRATION AND IMMIGRATION

During the 1800s and into the 1900s, the United States experienced mass immigration from many European countries. Of all the European immigrants during that period, the greatest proportion of any one country's population that headed west across the Atlantic was from Ireland. Norway was second. Overall, nearly one million Norwegians emigrated to the United States.

Emigration from Norway to the United States dates back to the early 1800s, when a group of Norwegian Quakers (a religious group) left Stavanger and found religious refuge in an area of New York close to Lake Ontario. Many friends and family members from the southwestern area of Norway followed, especially after the Norwegians in America began to migrate to the Midwest, where economic opportunities were more abundant at the time.

Emigration from Norway escalated rapidly during the 1860s, as discussed in the previous chapter, with most migrants coming from the rural areas of Norway. They left their homeland from the ports of Trondheim, Bergen, and Oslo, passed through Ellis Island in New York Harbor, and headed west to Chicago and points beyond in Minnesota, Wisconsin, Iowa, and the Dakotas. Norwegians, choosing to live with their relatives and friends, established dozens of rural towns in the Midwest and Great Plains. Norwegian emigration to the United

States came to a halt as the Great Depression settled in on the United States and the rest of the world during the 1930s.

It was not until after World War II that Norway began to experience immigration, and even then it was on a very small scale. Under 5 percent of the country's population is foreign-born. Not surprisingly the largest foreign-born populations are from Denmark and Sweden. In 2001, more than 57 percent of all immigrants to Norway came from Europe. Sweden provided over 13 percent of the immigrants and Denmark accounted for another 9 percent of the newcomers. Outside of Europe, Asia is the region that has provided the greatest number of immigrants, some 22 percent of the total. The majority of Asians come from Iraq and Pakistan.

Most foreign immigrants have settled in Oslo and the immediately surrounding communities. The government, however, has established reception centers throughout the country for the many refugees seeking asylum in Norway. As a result, every Norwegian county experienced a net growth in migration from abroad during 2001.

The longer an immigrant resides in Norway, the more likely the person is to be employed. One study discovered that the Norwegian industries in which immigrants work vary on the basis of home country or region. For instance, most foreign workers in Norway's gas and oil industry are from Europe, North America, and Oceania. In the service industries—such as hotels, restaurants, sanitation, and cleaning services—the vast majority of foreign workers come from Asia, Africa, and Latin America.

To become a citizen of Norway, one must live in the country for at least seven years before being eligible to apply for naturalization. If married to a Norwegian citizen, the person may apply for naturalization in four years. Although most migrants come to Norway from Europe, most of the migrants who apply for Norwegian citizenship come from non-Western countries. Many Europeans who migrate to Norway plan to return home eventually. In 2002, over 90 percent of migrants who became naturalized Norwegian citizens came from non-Western countries. Since 1977, when Norway began keeping statistics on naturalizations, Pakistan, Vietnam, Yugoslavia, and Turkey were the home countries of the largest number of new Norwegian citizens.

In 2001, 34,264 immigrants arrived in Norway and 26,309 Norwegians emigrated to other parts of the world. Europe drew more than 72 percent of Norwegian emigrants in 2001, with most going to Sweden and Denmark. Over 1,200 Norwegians migrated to Spain, largely to settle in retirement communities on the Mediterranean coast. The Americas received about 9 percent of Norwegian emigrants in 2001, the vast majority of them beccooming U.S. immigrants.

SAMI

Among Norway's 4.5 million people are some 40,000 Sami (formerly called "Lapps," or "Reindeer People"). The Sami are an indigenous group that has lived in the northern regions of Norway, Sweden, and Finland and the western part of Russia for more than 1,000 years. Across this space of the Scandinavian peninsula, Finland, and the Kola Peninsula of Russia live 75,000 Sami, but most live in far northern Norway. However, the largest concentration of Sami in one place is Oslo. There, about 5,000 Sami reside after having given up their rugged native lifestyle for the relative ease and comfort of urban life.

Over the last 400 years, Norway's policies toward the Sami have paralleled the policies of other Western nations toward their indigenous people. Just as the United States spent decades trying to assimilate American Indians, the Norwegians had a policy of assimilation toward the Sami that dated back to 1600. The first part of the Norwegian policy of assimilation occurred as Norwegians migrated into the northern part of the Scandinavian peninsula in the 1600s and 1700s. During this time, Norwegians tended to establish fishing villages along the northern coast, bringing with them their capitalist economy and the Church of Norway.

Capitalism changes the way most indigenous people function economically. In most traditional Sami settlements, people lived in communities and used resources, such as reindeer herds, communally. However, individuals began to claim ownership of the north's reindeer herds in the 1700s. In that century, political boundaries also were drawn, creating countries within regions. In 1751, in a document called the Lappekodicillen, the newly defined countries of this region recognized Sami rights to reindeer herding. This document was the first legal recognition of Sami rights.

Despite the formal recognition of Sami rights, the people continued to be subjected to the Norwegian policy of assimilation. In the 1800s, Norway established schools in Sami lands and banned the speaking of the Sami language in those schools. That policy continued in many schools until the 1950s. As in the United States, the Norwegian government took many Sami primary school children from their homes (without permission of Sami parents) and placed them in boarding schools or in foster homes in southern Norway under the policy of "Norwegianization." The assimilation policy also denied many Sami the right to own land. It also pressured the Sami to discontinue reindeer herding in favor of individual ownership of farms.

The Norwegian government significantly altered its policies toward the Sami following World War II, largely due to one of the first actions of the newly formed United Nations: the 1948 passage of the United Nations Declaration on Human Rights. Norway embraced this document, which recognized the fundamental rights of all people. During the 1950s, Norway began to study the conditions of the Sami and their rights. Just as the civil rights movement changed the condition of African Americans in the United States in the 1960s, the Sami people began to organize and demand their rights in the same decade. They were allowed to pursue their traditional economic way of life and encouraged to preserve their culture. They were given access to social and economic development programs and allowed to assemble their own government.

In 1988, Norway amended its constitution to incorporate Article 110a, which reads, "It is the responsibility of the authorities of the State to create conditions enabling the Sami people to preserve and develop its language, culture and way of life." With that action, any policies that actively promoted assimilation of the Sami ended. One year later, the first Sami Assembly (parliament) convened in Norway. In 1992, Norway passed the Sami Language Act, making Sami and Norwegian both official languages in certain parts of Norway that have large Sami populations.

While today Norway's policies tend toward preservation of Sami culture rather than assimilation, the policies of the last four hundred years certainly had a great impact. Today, for example, only about 10 percent of the Sami make a living from reindeer herding.

In the post–World War II era, the Sami began a cultural revival. Today, one sees the *kofte*, the traditional Sami clothes, more frequently both within and outside the northern Sami homeland. Similarly, Sami movies, publications, and music are now found throughout Norway. Mari Boine Persen, a Sami vocalist, is helping spread the Sami language with her songs that are hits throughout Scandinavia.

FESTIVALS

The greatest festivities of Norway's year fall on May 17, also called Syttende Mai, or Constitution Day. As mentioned earlier, this date in 1814 marks the date of the adoption of the Norwegian constitution, written after the dissolution of the Denmark-Norway union and just before the Sweden-Norway union. Each May 17, Norwegians celebrate Constitution Day with multiple events. In the morning, the observances are typically solemn occasions, held at war memorials and in state churches. In the afternoon, the events turn to a more celebratory tone, when Norwegians recognize the occasion with hundreds of parades. The parades are joyful events that celebrate the people of Norway and the society they have created. They occur throughout the country, from tiny villages to sprawling Oslo. In each community, the parades are open to everyone, but they are planned by committees representing local associations and political parties. Of the various community organizations responsible for planning the parades, two of the most common are sports clubs and Christian religious groups.

One parade held in each community that has a primary school is the children's parade. In a typical children's parade, each pupil carries a Norwegian flag, wearing either folk costumes or new clothes, and walks the parade route behind a school banner and school band. Children of recent immigrants to Norway will often dress in their native country's folk costume and march along with the rest of their school. While several adults walk with the children as chaperones, nearly all the participants in the children's parade are youngsters.

For nearly a century, Norway and Norwegians have prospered. The country, after centuries of turbulence, has found remarkable stability. One of several reasons helping to explain the present state of well-being enjoyed by these north-landers is good government. In the following chapter, you will learn about Norway's government, how it functions, and the ways in which the country's people benefit from its rule.

The Storting (Norwegian Parliament) is the most important government body created in the 1814 constitution.

5

Government

T he folk legend that most comes to mind when one considers the evolution of Norway's government is that of the Draugen and Ola, told at the beginning of this book. At the end of the story, the Draugen never returns to Ola's territory because his ancestors helped drive it away. When examining the political history of Norway, one must understand the impact of the relationships Norway has shared with its neighbors during the last six centuries. To recap, at one time, Norway dominated other lands, as was the case during the Viking period. By the end of the Middle Ages, Norway entered a union with Denmark that lasted 400 years. The union with Denmark ended in 1814 with the resolution of the Napoleonic Wars, when Sweden, who, during the wars, had worked to defeat Napoleon and was now in a position of power, wrested influence over Norway from Denmark. Norway continued in this union with Sweden until its formal independence in 1905. Even during the twentieth century Norway again experienced domination when Nazi Germany occupied the country during World War II.

During recent years, another union has been knocking on Norway's door—the European Union (EU). The EU has twice invited Norway to join their economic and political union, and twice the voters in Norway have rejected the invitation. Some analysts believe that Norway's reluctance to join the European Union stems from the country's relatively recent (1905) independence. Others point to Norwegians' strong sense of nationalism and their concern that their interests will be lost in the multitude of concerns and issues facing the European Union. Regardless of the underlying reason(s), Norway has chosen to maintain its political independence. It has, however, entered into a trade agreement with the EU while declining full membership. Norwegians, especially rural Norwegians (represented by the legendary Ola), are resistant to letting another political influence back into their territory.

SOCIAL WELFARE

One major difference sets the governments of Scandinavia (Norway, Sweden, Finland, and Denmark) apart from those of other countries in Western Europe: the level of commitment they have to the social welfare of their citizenry. All wealthy countries in the world have social welfare systems, such as health-care aid for the poor and social security for the retired. In Scandinavia, the level of commitment for the social welfare of the citizenry is enormous.

The Norwegian government built its social welfare system based on three principles. The first principle is universality, under which every Norwegian citizen has the right to access to social welfare programs. Whether a Norwegian is poor or rich, employed or not, he or she has the right to benefits such as maternity leave and access to free health care. One interesting geographic aspect of the principle of universality in Norway is that the government believes all its citizens should have access to social benefits, regardless of where they live. As a result, the Norwegian government ensures the provision of services in major cities such as Oslo and also in sparsely populated northern counties.

The second principle of Norway's social welfare system involves tying the provision of cash benefits to each citizen's income. For instance, a female corporate executive earning a high income would have maternity benefits with a high cash benefit. A woman who earns a low income as a waitress, on the other hand, receives a much lower level of maternity benefits, matching her regular income. Even unemployed women receive some cash maternity benefits, based on a proportion of the average production worker's wage. The Norwegian government believes that paid leave for infant care or for disability should not mean a large decline in a family's standard of living.

The final basic principle in the Norwegian social welfare system is that the state, rather than private individuals or agencies, should provide all essential social services. Most social services, including health care, education, and child and elderly care are provided by counties or municipalities. A few private companies do play a small role in providing some social services, but the Norwegian government funds even these companies.

Norway affords all of these social welfare projects through taxes based on income. Much of a typical Norwegian's income is paid in taxes, which are among the highest of any country. In return, citizens receive more benefits, "from cradle to grave," than do citizens of nearly any other country. Norwegians expect that future generations will likewise work and pay high income taxes to pay for their benefits, including income when they retire.

THE NORWEGIAN GOVERNMENT SYSTEM

The Storting (Norwegian parliament) is by far the most important body created in the 1814 constitution. It is the legislative power and has the responsibility of allocating state funds, of amending the constitution, and of passing laws. Norwegians elect the 165 members of the Storting every four years. Unlike other European states that can call for new elections at any time, Norway's constitution allows elections only every four years.

Norway's 19 counties serve as the electoral districts for Storting elections. The number of seats chosen from each county varies with population. Concerned with the geographic component of the principle of universality, the Norwegian government uniquely established an electoral system whereby the least populated counties receive more representation per voter in the Storting than do densely populated counties. Eight of the 165 seats are at-large, chosen to ensure proportionality between the votes cast for each political party and the number of seats each political party holds.

The Stortling's 165 members are divided into two chambers, the Odelsting (with 124 members) and the Lagting (with 41 members). A bill goes through several processes en route to becoming a law. First, members of government study it. The bill then enters the legislative process in the Odelsting. If passed by the Odelsting, the Lagting then considers it. If the Lagting approves it, the bill continues on for signing by the king and the prime minister.

Political parties are represented proportionally between the Odelsting and the Lagting. As a result, the Lagting acts solely as a check on the Odelsting, to ensure the Storting passes good legislation. During its first century of modern independence, the Labour Party was the most powerful in Norwegian politics. That is changing today, as the Conservatives, the Party of Progress, the Socialist Left, and the Christian Democrats challenged the supremacy of the Labour Party in the 2001 Storting elections.

If no one political party is the clear winner of a Storting election, two or more parties will enter an agreement to create a government, choosing the prime minister and the ministers of Norway's ministries (including agriculture, petroleum and energy, and the environment). These ministers compose the council of state, which is part of the executive power of the Norwegian government. The executive power is composed of the king in council.

The king serves as the formal head of state. In this capacity, he meets with foreign dignitaries and represents Norway internationally. His political powers regarding legislation are quite weak in practice. Although the king has the authority to veto legislation the Storting passes, only once has that happened since independence in 1905 (and in that case, the Storting asked him to do so). Within Norway, the king represents the government during national crises, during changes in government, and in everyday life.

The constitution describes the monarchy as hereditary and limited. This means that the king is chosen through specific succession rules outlined in the constitution. Since 1990, these rules have allowed for the succession of a woman to the throne, though no woman has served yet. The monarchy is also considered limited because at any point the Storting can amend the constitution to dissolve the monarchy.

In addition to the Storting and the monarchy, the constitution outlines a role for the Norwegian courts, the judiciary power. The highest court in the land, however, was not outlined in the constitution. Rather, a Royal resolution established the Supreme Court in 1815. The Supreme Court includes a president and 17 justices, 5 of whom sit for a given case. Below the Supreme Court are five high courts and approximately 100 urban and rural district courts. Each of the courts, from the district courts through the Supreme Court, hears civil and criminal cases.

Although not outlined in the constitution, Storting laws

have created, in practice, a major role for local government in Norway. Within counties and municipalities, local governments carry out much of the legislation the Storting passes. Specifically, the local governments are responsible for providing health care, child and elderly care, and education. This responsibility creates a multitude of government jobs at the local scale. Local governments employ an estimated one in five Norwegian workers.

THE EUROPEAN UNION

The European Union is a group of European countries that have opened their borders to each other for free movement of goods and people. It began in the 1950s as the European Steel and Coal Community and included Belgium, the Netherlands, Luxembourg, France, Germany, and Spain. These six countries agreed to allow the free flow of coal and steel across their borders, meaning no taxes, tariffs, or quotas. This agreement helped industries find inexpensive coal and steel resources, regardless of what resources were located within one country's borders.

Over the last five decades, this small group grew to become the European Economic Community and more recently the European Union in 1992. Members of the European Union are economically joined. This means that regulations for everything from pesticide use on crops, to additives in foods, to safety regulations on assembly lines mesh across country borders. In the last two decades, the European Union has stretched its agreements across country borders to encompass political questions such as foreign policy, immigration, and even the future development of a rapid reaction force (a police/military entity).

To join the European Union, a country expresses its interest to the EU governing body. Then, the European Union and the country undertake a lengthy, thorough study of whether the country is in fact ready for membership. Once the country makes necessary changes to its laws and practices, the European Union invites the country to join. The final say on joining the European Union rests in the hands of the citizens of the country. The country holds a referendum in which the citizens vote on whether to join.

Norway has held two such referendums, in 1972 and in 1994. In both elections, the vote was against EU membership. In 1972, 53.5 percent of Norwegians voted against joining. With heavy voter turn out in 1994, a slightly smaller number, 52.2 percent, also voted against membership.

The distribution of support for European Union membership had a clear geographical distribution in the 1994 vote. The counties and municipalities in the central-eastern part of the country, including Oslo, voted in favor of membership. Support for membership declined the farther north one traveled. Both the "yes" and "no" campaigns worked diligently to bring Norwegian voters into their camp. The "yes" campaign stressed that Norway's economy was tied into the European Union and that membership would give the country a voice over issues such as regulations that were already affecting them through trade. Norwegians in favor of membership saw direct representation in the European Union as an effective way to yield more political influence in Europe. Additionally, the "yes" campaign stressed the importance of the European Union's role in creating peace and security in Europe and the world.

The "no" campaign argued that if Norway joined the European Union it would lose sovereignty, meaning the Norwegian government would lose the final authority over what happens within its borders. Another argument against membership was the economic cost. The wealthiest members pay the most into the European Union, and Norwegians feared they would pay much more than they would receive in benefits.

Perhaps the strongest argument against membership was the fear of decline in the country's rural areas. This fear is evident in the fact that counties with the lowest population density were most strongly opposed to membership in the union. Norwegians, especially rural Norwegians, feared that as part of the European Union, focus on the rural areas of Norway would wane, particularly in the principle of universal access to services, whether rural or urban.

Ironically, the rural areas of Norway would be eligible for certain economic development funds were Norway to join the European Union. One of the major principles of the European Union is to funnel development (especially transportation and communication improvement) funds into the poorer areas of member countries. Nonetheless, the Norwegians in the rural areas felt they would fare better under the universality principle of the Norwegian government than under the European Union.

The areas of Norway that voted in favor of membership are those already most closely tied into Europe economically, politically, and culturally. Similarly, the areas of Finland and Sweden that most strongly supported their membership in the European Union were also the southern, urban areas.

NORWAY AND THE WORLD

For centuries, the Norwegian government has struggled with its role as an independent country and its role within the global community. Certainly today Norway is well integrated into the global capitalist economy. Despite its abstention from membership in the EU, Norway continues to be a major political player in the world and contributes a large proportion of its budget to foreign aid.

As another indicator of Norway's global impact, the Norwegian Storting annually chooses the winner of the Nobel Peace Prize, an honor that in fact stems from one of the country's several unions with outside powers. Among politically conscious citizens of the globe, the most coveted award is the Nobel Peace Prize. Established by Alfred Nobel, a Swedish scientist in the late 1800s, the prize is one of several awarded annually, including a number in science and literature.

During Nobel's time, Norway and Sweden were in a union. As a Swede, Nobel assigned the task of choosing the prize winners in science and literature to Swedish organizations. However, he specifically stated that the Norwegian Storting, in existence since 1814, was to have the responsibility of choosing the Nobel Peace Prize winner. Thus a committee chosen by the Storting selects the winner and awards the prize on December 10 each year.

Bergen is the chief city and seaport of Western Norway. For more than 500 years it was the country's largest urban center, only yielding its place to Oslo in the nineteenth century.

6

Economy

M any Norwegian folktales offer simple explanations as to why creatures look the way they do. For instance, the fox has a white tip on its tail because he tried to steal butter, knocking over a churn and splashing his tail with cream as he ran off. Or, the bear has a short tail because he was sitting on ice one day ice fishing when the ice froze around his tail. When he quickly rose to catch a fish, he pulled off his tail. When explaining a country's economy, it is tempting to offer simple explanations for why conditions are as they are—why, for example, one country is poor while another is rich. With Norway, it would be simple to say that the country appears rich because of its oil and natural gas resources. However, the explanation offered in this chapter goes well beyond this simple reality. Several factors are presented to explain how Norway has become one of the world's most wealthy countries, how it developed a remarkable standard of living for its people, and how it plans to maintain this wealth and standard of living in the future.

Norway's economy is part of the global capitalist economy in which all the world's countries participate. Some countries, such as the Soviet Union when it existed, chose systems in which the government plays a huge role in the economy, creating state capitalism. In a state capitalist system, the government owns most of the land. It also owns most factories and other means of production and determines what, where, how, and by whom things will be produced. In the same vein, the state economy is still tied into the global economy because the state buys, sells, and trades goods in the same world markets as do other countries. On the other end of the global economy spectrum are states in which government plays a small role in ownership, production, or regulation of companies. Countries such as the United States and Norway fall between these two extremes. A country's gross domestic product (GDP) provides some insight into how involved a country's government is with economic production. For instance, 32.8 percent of the American gross domestic product comes from government expenditures. In Norway, however, 55.5 percent of the Norwegian gross domestic product comes from government expenditures. This means that in Norway, the government plays a much more important role in creating the national economy than is the case in the United States.

THE TRADITIONAL ECONOMY

Economic activity in Norway ranges from very traditional pursuits, such as fishing and reindeer herding, to contemporary "postindustrial" activities. Traditional activities often are referred to as "primary industries." These include herding, fishing, farming, forestry, and mining.

Reindeer Herding

Traditional economic activities date back to the first human occupants of the Scandinavian peninsula. Ancestors of

Reindeer pull a sleigh carrying a group of Sami. Today the Sami people tend about 200,000 head of domesticated reindeer.

the Sami followed reindeer herds to northern Norway following the end of the Ice Age. Today, the Sami are still the chief inhabitants of this environmentally harsh region. Their economy continues to be culturally centered on reindeer, though much has changed in recent decades.

Domestication (transition from wild to tamed for human use) changed the relationship between the Sami and reindeer. Initially, reindeer were hunted only. With domestication, they became herd animals, much like cattle or sheep. Today, an estimated 200,000 head of domesticated reindeer live in the Sami herds, are privately owned, and are raised through purposeful grazing, much as livestock in the rest of the Western world. Only about 20,000 head of reindeer continue to live in "wild" reindeer herds.

In the 1970s, the Norwegian Ministry of Agriculture and the Sami Reindeer Herders' Association reached a series of agreements relative to the reindeer business. Today, the Sami have exclusive control over reindeer herding, based upon traditional practices and rules. Sami herds graze over vast areas of northern and central Norway, inhabiting an estimated 40 percent of the country. Most of the land used for herding is in Finnmark County located in the extreme north.

Reindeer herding is fully integrated into Sami life and is essential to the survival of their culture. Recent changes in the reindeer economy, however, are causing some serious economic and environmental concerns. Modern technologies such as the snowmobile have been brought into the herding process. Emphasis is now on production and profit. Reindeer numbers are extremely high and serious overgrazing is occurring. Many political players, including the Ministry of Agriculture, county and community agencies, the Sami Assembly, and the Sami Reindeer Herders' Association, are worried about the survival of the industry.

Fishing

In addition to reindeer herding, Norway's traditional economy has always depended upon fishing, sealing, and (until recently) whaling since humans arrived on the Scandinavian peninsula. Norway's physical geography makes it extremely favorable to the fishing industry. The North Sea, the Barents Sea, the Norwegian Sea, and a heavily fjorded coast surround much of the country. These areas are among the most favorable and productive fishing grounds in the world.

The Norwegian fish catch is quite diverse. In value, the most important species are cod, herring, mackerel, prawn (shrimp), and haddock. Other important species are blue whiting, sand eel, ling, halibut, redfish, and tusk. Although both private fishermen and companies are heavily invested in and dependent upon fishing, the government strictly regulates this economic activity.

Norway's fishing fleet includes more than 13,500 primarily private vessels. Vessels range is size from small one-person fishing boats called *sjarks* that are found in the fjords, to massive trawlers capable of processing the fish while at sea. Catching such a large variety of sea life requires diverse means. Fishers use various kinds of nets, lines, seines, and trawls to make their catch.

Seals and whales also are taken by Norway's fishing industry, but only within established managed limits. Seals and minke whale populations are constantly monitored and the harvest is determined on this basis. Special efforts also are made to ensure that the animals are caught humanely and efficiently.

Norway is in a unique position to expand the importance of its fishing economy in the future. In today's world, food from the sea is becoming increasingly important. Fish farms and aquaculture are expanding rapidly around the world. With its fjorded coast and tens of thousands of rivers and lakes, Norway is geographically ready to move into expanded production. Fish farming and aquaculture are already a growing segment of the country's fishing economy. All indications are that they will only grow in importance in the future. Today, fish farming tends to focus on salmon and trout, with halibut, catfish, and a variety of shellfish beginning to become important.

Norway is committed to protecting the future of its fishing industry. The country established a 200-nautical-mile exclusive economic zone around its coastal borders to protect its claims and rights to valuable fishing grounds. It also entered agreements with neighboring countries to protect species, establish quotas, and manage fisheries. The government is interested in marine research, in furthering the industry, in protecting the environment, and in planning for a better future for the fishing industry.

Norway views fishing as a renewable resource. It also recognizes that the fishing industry is the second-largest segment of its export economy and it must be sustained. About 90 percent of the catch that reaches Norway's shore ends up as export products. In an average year, the value of exported fish products ranges between $3 to $4 billion. Over half the fish export goes to European Union countries. When properly managed, fishing provides Norway with economic stability and facilitates potential for future growth.

Agriculture

Agriculture in Norway is severely limited by the shortage of arable (farmable) land. Cultural practices of inheritance also have made it difficult for agriculture to efficiently thrive. Thus Norway has long had to rely on imports to maintain an adequate supply of food. Today, these issues continue to affect the agricultural economy of Norway.

The principal agricultural problem is a lack of land. Only about 2,500,000 acres (1 million hectares), or 4 percent, of Norway's land is suitable for agriculture. Approximately one-third of that land is farmed, the remainder being used as meadow or pastureland. In this limited amount of space, farmers must produce as much food as possible to meet the needs of the Norwegian people. This is a difficult task.

Traditional inheritance practices also made it difficult for farmers to produce efficiently on Norway's arable lands. For hundreds of years, tradition decreed that when a landowner died, his lands were to be distributed equally to all his sons. Eventually, the population grew to a point where people were forced to move elsewhere to obtain land. In modern times, landowners usually leave the land to the oldest son. While this tradition has kept the farm together, other children have had to leave the land. This practice has encouraged migration to urban areas within Norway and emigration from the country.

Norway is able to produce approximately half of its needed

food supply. On those occasions during the nineteenth and twentieth centuries when the country was cut off from trade with neighboring countries, many Norwegians suffered from severe food shortages resulting in widespread famine.

Today, the principal grain crops in order of importance are barley, oats, and wheat. Grain production really centers on several small areas in southeastern Norway that, together, account for almost two-thirds of the country's grain production. Some oil-seed and pea production accompanies grain production in these areas. Other crops include potatoes, root crops, vegetables, rye grass, and other crops for fodder and silage (fodder converted to livestock feed).

In recent years, Norway has been somewhat successful in efforts to increase its meadow and pasture area. Meadows are mowed for hay and pastures are grazed. Meadows and pastures tend to be located in the more rugged mountain and plateau areas of the country.

Southeastern Norway contains the best agricultural lands. Most of the good soils are found in the river valleys descending toward the sea. A second area of agricultural lands is in the river valleys extending to the fjorded west coast. These agricultural lands provide much of the food supply for Norway's livestock industry. Principal animals are cattle (including dairy cows), sheep, oxen, pigs, dairy goats, and horses. Reindeer in the extreme north account for only about 1 percent of the livestock economy. Norway also has a poultry industry with over three million chickens raised for egg and meat production. The livestock industry not only uses most of the agricultural land, but also accounts for most of the agricultural income.

As is happening in the United States, Norway is experiencing a continuous decline in the number of farms. Farms have declined from about 200,000 in 1960 to slightly more than 75,000 in 2000. In Norway, as in the United States, fewer and fewer farmers and their families earn their living from farming

Norwegians raking hay in a pasture near Hardangerfjord. Meadows and pasture tend to be located in the more rugged mountain and plateau areas.

alone. In fact, in Norway, the majority of farmers earn less than half of their income from farming.

Forestry

Forest-related industries provide employment for over 30,000 people, primarily in rural areas of the country. About one-fourth of the people engaged in forest industries own the land they work. Needleleaf coniferous evergreen trees account for over 90 percent of the harvest. Coniferous trees have excellent qualities that make them valuable for both sawn lumber and wood fiber products.

About one-half the wood cut in Norway goes to saw mills where it is processed for construction materials. The variety of lumber materials and uses has increased in recent years with the growth of laminated, glue-laminated, and engineered wood products. In recent years, Norway has experienced an increase in the export of wooden products. Over half of the people employed in the forest industry work within this sector of the forest economy.

The other major user of forest products is the pulp and paper industry. Norway produces paper and board products, wood pulp, and chemical pulp. Major products include newsprint and higher grades of paper for export, packing paper, wood pulp, and chemical pulp. The latter is used in a variety of products including manufactured fibers.

One of the most significant areas of impact of the forest industry on Norway is in transportation. Over one-third of all railroad traffic is related to forest products. About 15 percent of the highway and road traffic is based on the movement of forest products to mills and markets. Finally, sea transportation is the primary means for moving forest products to foreign markets.

Mining

Norway's mining sector includes industrial minerals, building stone and construction materials, metallic minerals, and mineral fuels. By far the most important of Norway's minerals are the fossil fuels, as they have a wide-ranging effect on the whole country. The rest of the mineral economy is primarily of local importance.

Norway's major industrial minerals include dolomite, olivine, and syenite. The country is one of the world's major producers of olivine, an important mineral in iron and steel processing, foundry sands, abrasives, roofing tiles, and lasers. Syenite is used in making glass products and industrial ceramics.

Building stone and construction materials also are important to the mining economy. Dimension stones, limestone, sand, and gravel dominate production, value, and employment. Dimension stones, including granite, gneiss, marble, flagstone, and slate, comprise Norway's principal building and monument minerals. Particularly important is larvikite. This blue granite stone from the Larvik area in southeastern Norway has become an important exterior building stone that also is exported. Another product, Norwegian rose marble, is quarried in the north. Quartzite and slate quarries are located in the central and northern parts of the country and provide materials for the monument and construction industries. Other construction minerals such as aggregate, limestone, sand and gravel, crushed rock, and clay are important to the building and transportation segments of the economy.

While a variety of metallic minerals are found in Norway, including ilmenite, iron ore, copper, zinc, lead, gold, and nickel, mining of metallic ores has declined significantly in recent years. Metallic mining focuses primarily on ilmenite (iron titanium oxide) and iron ore. Ilmenite is processed in Tyssedal and is used in a variety of manufactured products including paints, plastics, and paper. Local effects of iron ore production are evident in places such as Mo-I-Rana along the west coast and near the Arctic Circle, where Rautaruukki Steel produces rolled and welded steel products.

Contemporary mining for metals focuses primarily on iron ore, such as in this iron mine in Kirkennes, Norway.

While Norway is rich in petroleum and natural gas, it has few other mineral fuels. Norway's coal is concentrated in the remote northern islands of Svalbard. Much of the coal is used to generate electrical power. The lack of coal on the peninsula caused Norway to look elsewhere for fuels prior to the development of petroleum economy. Although wood is not a mineral, it was the main source of fuel for Norway for many centuries. Similarly, hydropower (again not a mineral) has become a major energy source since the industrial revolution.

THE MODERN ECONOMY

Today, Norway's economy is diverse and strong. Much of its strength is based on its diversity. When one sector of the economy sags because of fluctuations in the international market, or some other factor, other sectors can pick up the slack.

Manufacturing

Norway has a well-developed manufacturing economy. Manufacturing began initially with the building of boats, weapons, and tools, and the smoking and salting of fish. Over time, it grew, became increasingly diversified, and today includes many high-tech industries. Historically, much of the manufacturing centered on the processing of Norway's own natural resources. Today, much of the processing involves resources and raw materials that are imported.

Manufacturing benefits tremendously from Norway's position as a major supplier of low-cost power. For over a century, the country has produced an abundance of low-cost hydroelectric power. In recent decades, coal from Svalbard and offshore petroleum and natural gas have provided Norway with additional low-cost power access along its west coast.

Norway's most important industry is food processing. This industry includes the processing of seafood products from the fishing industry, of meat from livestock, of dairy products from cows and goats, and of eggs and poultry products. Other food products include processed vegetables, fruits, juices, and jams. Norway also produces beer and soft drinks using barley, local waters, and other additives, and coffee using imported beans obtained on the world market.

During the dawn of the Industrial Revolution in Europe in the 1800s, most industries relied on coal for power. Since Norway's coal resources are from its remote far northern islands, the country turned to an energy source located abundantly throughout the land: moving water. At the turn of the twentieth century, Norsk Hydro began using hydro power to produce fertilizer. Today, a large segment of Norway's manufacturing production is closely related to the availability of clean and inexpensive hydroelectric power. For example, over one-third of the hydroelectric power produced is used in the metal, chemical, and wood product industries. Industries that use hydroelectric power are somewhat flexible in location. Some may be located close to the power source, others near the raw materials, and still others in urban centers or port cities.

A growing segment of the manufacturing economy closely related to cheap power availability is the light metals industry. Norway has produced aluminum for over 100 years. It also produces magnesium, silicon, and other light metals. This industry was started simply to process local and imported ores. Over time, it has grown and expanded to more advanced processing of these products. A good example of this is the aluminum extrusion industry, which takes aluminum ingots and extrudes them into a variety of shapes and sizes. These in turn have led to the manufacturing of still other metal products such as windows, doors, building materials, and auto parts. There are numerous light metal manufacturing facilities in Norway, centered in Oslo, Havil, Magnor, and Sunndalsøra.

Production of transportation and mechanical engineering equipment is another major manufacturing category. This includes the building of ships, fishing vessels, hulls, pleasure boats, and related repair industries. It also includes the manufacturing of submersible drilling platforms for the petroleum economy, buoys, beacons, landing stages, and other floating structures. Also included in transportation is the manufacturing of truck, bus, motor coach, dump and delivery truck bodies, and tractors. Manufacturing centers for these products include Oslo, Bergen, Aker, Lysaker, and Horten.

Petroleum and Natural Gas

Norway's petroleum economy is the primary source of the country's present position as a world economic power. Extensive petroleum and natural gas deposits were discovered on Norway's continental shelf in the North Sea in 1969. Of the two, petroleum is by far the most important. Almost 80 percent of this sector's production is petroleum, with natural gas accounting for the remaining 20 percent. Combined, their present production exceeds US $25 billion a year. This amounts to over 23 percent of the Norwegian gross domestic product and as much as 35 percent of its exports. Norway ranks third after Saudi Arabia and Russia in oil and gas exports. The Ekofisk district, the primary production area, is located in the North Sea. Portions of the original field were idled and production expanded to the Ekofisk II district in the late 1990s. Production should continue here for another 40 to 50 years. Other major oil-fields include Statfjord, Gullfak, and Oseberg. The major natural gas field is Troll in the Norwegian Sea. Additionally, new oil and gas fields continue to be developed and opened. New production sites on the vast Norwegian continental shelf extend under the Norwegian Sea, and exploration is also occurring in the Barents Sea.

Petroleum and natural gas are moved to refineries and markets by pipelines and tankers. Petroleum is piped from the offshore platforms to terminals at Mongstad and Sture in Norway and at Teeside in the United Kingdom. Natural gas is piped from the wells to terminals at Kårstø and Tjeldbergodden in Norway and also directly to Scotland, Belgium, France, and Germany. Today, Norway controls about one-half of Europe's oil and gas reserves. It also provides about 20 percent of Western Europe's natural gas needs.

The petroleum economy has had a tremendous impact on Norway. It has stimulated the manufacture and sale of equipment used in oil and gas exploration, production, and distribution. Additionally, activities related to the industry have created thousands of jobs in government, manufacturing, and in the petroleum and natural gas industries. It has also furthered Norway's social democratic governmental policies.

This platform was the world's largest natural gas platform when it was towed in April 2000 from a shipyard in Stavanger in the first stage of its journey to a North Sea destination. Today, Norway controls one-half of Europe's oil and natural gas reserves.

Petroleum and natural gas industries, production, and distribution are controlled by government enterprises. There are some efforts to privatize as much as one-third of

Statoil, the state-owned oil company. The government would add profits from such a sale to the Government Petroleum Fund, which is Norway's plan for providing ongoing monies for the country's social program needs once petroleum and gas production expires. This fund is growing rapidly. The value is approaching US $75 billion and is expected to quickly move on toward $100 billion. Norway invests the fund's monies worldwide.

Banking and Trade

Norway is growing in importance as a banking center. Its growth has been stimulated by the impact of the petroleum economy and the development of the Government Petroleum Fund. The Norges Bank is located in Oslo. It manages all monetary policies and sets all interest rates. The basic unit of currency is the Norwegian Krone.

Some aspects of banking in Norway may appear different to the average American bank user. Banking includes full-service banks, savings banks, commercial banks, merchant banks, specialized banks, and even the post office. Specialized banks focus on just one industry, for example. There are specialized banks for the fishing industry, manufacturing, shipping, home construction, and even exporters. Only recently Norway allowed foreign banks to operate in the country. Presently, two American banks, Citibank International and Chase Manhattan Bank Norge, operate in Norway.

Norway's primary trading partners are the members of the European Union. Almost 77 percent of its exports go to EU countries including, in order of importance, the United Kingdom, France, Germany, the Netherlands, and Sweden. An additional 8 percent of its exports go to the United States.

Tourism

Norway is a spectacular place to visit. The Norwegian Tourist Board is making a major effort to entice foreign visitors and to increase the profitability of travel-related businesses. Today, some three to four million foreigners visit Norway each year, resulting in the employment of over 125,000 people and the addition of about US $3 billion to the nation's economy. During recent years, major investments have been made to upgrade the tourism infrastructure. This has resulted in improvements in roads, port facilities, airports, lodging, and such recreational amenities as golf courses and ski lifts.

One of Norway's most important tourist attractions is its people. Norwegians are wonderful about making foreign visitors feel welcome. Visitors of Norwegian descent are especially happy to see their ancestral homeland and search for relatives.

Norway provides tourists with spectacular natural scenery and sightseeing, historic communities, homes, churches, museums, amusement parks, shopping, and a wide variety of cultural attractions. It offers the visitor excellent transportation, motor coach tours, clean and comfortable accommodations, and quality dining. It also offers tremendous winter recreation opportunities, fishing, boat tours, as well as the chance to visit Sami cultural areas.

Transportation and Communication

Norway's transportation infrastructure is changing rapidly. Historically, the country has had poor roads, limited railroad development outside mining and port areas, and simple airports. The huge distance from north to south and the country's rugged terrain (including the east-west-extending coastal fjords) have combined to make travel between northern and southern locations difficult and costly.

Norway has 56,656 miles (91,180 kilometers) of highways. Almost 75 percent of them are paved. Recent efforts to improve the infrastructure of Norway have led to extensive efforts to tunnel through the mountains, shorten roads, improve the safety of travelers and truckers, and facilitate travel between urban and rural areas. Norway now has 67.7 miles (109 kilometers) of urban expressway.

Railroads in Norway operate on 2,493 miles (4,012 kilometers) of standard gauge track. Of that total, 1,572 miles (2,530 kilometers) of track are electrified. Most railroad engines are also electric. Railroads link mining and forest areas with processing and export centers. They also connect major urban areas and some urban centers with scenic areas.

Norway has developed three major airports, two of which are in the Oslo area. Gardermoen Airport, located 30 miles (50 kilometers) north of Oslo, is the country's primary facility. Buses and trains connect Gardermoen with Oslo. The other airport in the Oslo area is Torp, located in Sandefjord, about 65 miles (104 kilometers) from the capital. The third major airport is at Bergen, located some 12 miles (19 kilometers) south of the city. There are 100 other smaller airports in Norway.

Water transportation is also important. As a land surrounded on three sides by coasts and with many sheltered fjords, Norway has numerous ports. Major port cities are Oslo, Bergen, Trondheim, Stavanger, and Kristiansand. Norway has 764 ships in its merchant marine, with about one-third of the fleet being petroleum and liquefied gas tankers. Ships from Norway sail to ports throughout the world.

Norway has developed an excellent telecommunications infrastructure. There are over 2.7 million telephone lines and more than two million mobile cellular telephones. The country has numerous radio (655) and television (360) stations. It also ranks among the top countries in the world for Internet access. Over half the people in Norway have Internet access through 13 service providers.

As has been mentioned, Norwegians enjoy one of the world's highest standards of living. The government plays an important role in ensuring the well-being of its citizens.

During recent decades, Norway's petroleum and natural gas reserves have helped make the country one of the wealthiest in the world. The development of this sector also fuels the government's social welfare programs, urges growth in the banking and financial sectors, affects industrial location in the manufacturing sector, and provide an economic safety network for the traditional economy.

More than 200 babies and their parents came together in Frogneparken Café in Oslo on June 22, 2000. They were celebrating a WHO (World Health Organization) study that found Norway scored as one of the best countries in the world when it came to medical care for infants.

7

Living in Norway Today

Among the numerous characters in Norwegian folktales and mythic legends, the most important are the Haugfolket. Norwegians use several different names to refer to these groups of people who live underground, in the mountains, and in the hills. Legend has it that when God visited Eve one day, many of her children were presentable, but others were messy. She asked the messy children to hide and showed only her presentable children to God. In response, God proclaimed that what is hidden shall remain hidden. The descendents of these hidden children are the Haugfolket. Norwegians see the Haugfolket as inferior to humans who do not live hidden lives. The Haugfolket, though living in hidden places, make their livings as do other Norwegians, fishing and farming.

The stories of the Haugfolket parallel the lives of Norwegians during different eras of occupation and domination over the last seven centuries. Norwegians led "hidden" lives, where their language, religion, government, and economy were controlled by outside forces. Despite this, Norwegians clung to their identity as a group and walked among their occupiers. In the last century, the "hidden" Norwegians have come to rule the land and have revived their own culture.

LANGUAGE

Historically, as early as 200 A.D., the Vikings had a runic alphabet (derived from Greek and Latin and used by Germanic peoples) that originally consisted of 24 letters. The Vikings used a combination of runic letters and pictures carved into wood and stone to tell stories of heroic adventures, to communicate with others, to write love letters, to record bills, and to keep calendars.

Some 700 to 1,000 years ago, as the Viking era was ending, most Scandinavian people spoke a language known as Old Norse, or North Germanic. All related to Old Norse, the modern Norwegian, Danish, and Swedish languages are contemporary variations of the North Germanic language. If a person can speak or read one of the three, chances are he or she would be able to function comfortably in the other two languages.

Contemporary Norway is the home to four important languages, three of which are "Norwegian" and one of which is unrelated: Bokmål, Nynorsk, Samnorsk, and Sami.

Bokmål, also known as Dano-Norwegian, is the official language of Norway. Norwegians refer to it as the "book language," because it is commonly the language of written publications, business transactions, and government. It is the primary language of eastern Norway.

The second major language in Norway is Nynorsk, also called Landsmål or New Norwegian. Following Norwegian independence, linguist Ivar Aasen developed Nynorsk as a reflection of the new nationalism, basing it on the dialects of the rural countryside. It is the primary language in the southern and western areas of the country.

Another version of Norwegian, Samnorsk, is a combination of Bokmål and Nynorsk and is spoken in urban communities. With more people speaking Samnorsk, rural dialects are disappearing quickly.

The Sami people of the north speak several dialects of a common language closely related to Finnish. However, the spoken dialects of the Sami are so distinct that people in different geographic areas of the Sami lands do not understand each other. Their language survived serious governmental efforts to eliminate it through assimilation policies. In the first half of the twentieth century, further government actions expanded efforts to eliminate the Sami language. Following World War II, as government policies toward the Sami changed, efforts to supplant their language stopped.

RELIGION

Like languages, religions in Norway have also changed significantly since Viking times. The Viking peoples worshiped several gods. The most important were Odin, Thor, and Frey. Odin was the god of power and knowledge. Thor was a warrior god, and Frey and his sister Freyja were gods of fertility. They lived in the Viking's heaven known as Valhalla with heroes of battle. Warrior women known as Valkyries carried fallen Viking warriors from earth to happiness in Valhalla.

In the eleventh century, King Olav II established Christianity in Norway, ordering the Norwegian people to choose baptism or die. Following Olav II's death, a man touched his corpse and, according to legend, his wounds miraculously healed. Other miracles followed, leading to his canonization as Saint Olav in the Roman Catholic Church. Today, despite the Protestant Reformation, Saint Olav is still the patron saint of Norway.

In the mid-sixteenth century, the Protestant Reformation swept Norway. Danish king Christian III forced the change to Protestantism in Norway, which for several hundred years essentially required everyone to be a member of the church. The impact of that action is still evident in Norway, where the Church of Norway (affiliated with the Evangelical Lutheran church) is the official religion of the land. Some 86 percent of the population belongs to this faith. Members of other Protestant denominations and the Roman Catholic Church comprise another 3 percent of the population. Another 1 percent identify themselves as members of other religions and some 10 percent claim no religious affiliation. The assimilation policy of the twentieth century, along with missionary activities in the north, converted many Sami to Christianity. Other Sami still practice their traditional religion.

Norway's constitution designates the Church of Norway as the state religion. The king is the head of the church and appoints most of the religious leaders. Government monies pay for the operation of the church, including salaries, maintenance, and construction. Norwegian schools teach the values of the Church of Norway. Students who do not belong to that church attend alternative classes during periods of religious instruction.

EDUCATION

A basic tenet of Norway is equal education for all children regardless of place, socioeconomic class, or need. Public education is provided free to all children, who must attend school from ages 6 through 16 years. In Norway, students enter the school system when they are 6 years old. Their mandatory 10 years of schooling is comprised of three levels: the lower primary grades include grades one through four; the upper primary grades include grades five through seven; and the lower secondary school includes grades eight through ten. The government provides day care for lower-primary-grade students before and after school.

While some Sami still practice their traditional religion, many have converted to Christianity. These young Sami men are being blessed by a Christian clergyman.

Upper secondary education follows grade 10. It is comprised of three paths: theoretical education, vocational training, or partial qualification (a combination of theoretical and vocational education). Upper secondary offers basic foundation courses and apprenticeships to prepare students to enter higher education.

Curriculum from grade 1 on is determined by the national government. It consists of a core curriculum, Sami culture, religion, Norwegian language (either Bokmål or Nynorsk as determined by the local municipality), mathematics, social science, science and environment, arts, music, home economics, physical education, and English. Additionally, all students must obtain greater depth in Norwegian or English, take an additional foreign language, or study Norwegian sign language.

The government, school systems, parents, and pupils work closely together to meet the special education needs of individual students. Recent immigration into Norway has brought a large number of students speaking non-Norwegian languages. The government has made available programs and funds to enable all students to learn within their new educational environment.

Students earn access to higher education through success in the upper secondary schools. The country's four universities include the University of Oslo, which is the largest and oldest. Specialized universities focusing on disciplines such as agriculture, social science, business, architecture, and veterinary science, also educate the population. The National Institutes of Art are located at Bergen and Oslo. Additionally, 26 state university colleges located across Norway offer two- to four-year programs in technology, teacher training, engineering, health sciences, social work, and university core courses.

While approximately 900,000 students are attending primary and secondary schools and colleges and universities, another one million adults take courses through lifelong learning programs. These programs are designed to enhance individual competencies and improve career choices. Courses can be taken at local schools, at work, or via distance education (computer or television).

Private school education in Norway is a rarity. Only 1.7 percent of the primary and lower secondary students attend private schools. In fact, there are fewer than a hundred such private schools in the country and their enrollments are considerably lower than those of public schools. There is an ongoing political debate in the Storting about the status and increasing funding for private, or "freestanding" schools, as they are also called. Many of the freestanding schools are Steiner, Montessori, or Christian sect schools. The few private universities in Norway have little impact on the country's total higher education programming.

LITERATURE

In modern times, world-renowned Norwegian literature has joined the oral sagas of the Viking era. Norway is home to three Nobel Laureates: Henrik Ibsen, Knut Hamsun, and Sigrid Undset. It is also home to numerous other noted authors, including Dag Solstad, Cathrine Grøndahl, and Lisbet Hilde, and poets Olav H. Hauge, Rolf Jacobsen, and Bertrand Besigye. Particularly important today is the work of Jostein Gaarder, the author of *Sophie's World*. This work about a 14-year-old girl seeking to know who she is has become a world of its own. The book has sold 15 million copies in over 40 languages; it also became both a movie and television series.

FILM

Norway has a long-established film industry. However, while it produces quality films for local and regional markets, unlike neighboring Sweden it is not a major player in the world's film industry. Norway's films often reflect the literary accomplishments of its noted authors. They also reflect nature and the environment, often dealing with life in the north, the mountains, or on the sea. More recently, films have focused on the challenges of growing up in Norway. The most famous example of such youth-oriented films is *Sophie's World*.

MUSIC AND DANCE

Traditional music and dance developed together in Norway. The music encompasses certain instruments and the dance centers on the sounds and beats produced by the

Tourists are treated to a display of traditional folk music and dance at the open air museum in Voss, Norway.

instruments. The lur, a long bronze horn, is the traditional instrument of Norway. Other traditional instruments include the fiddle, the Hardanger fiddle, harp, langeleik (similar to a dulcimer), horn, flute, accordion, and clarinet.

Prior to 1800, bygdedans, or country dances, were the most important form of dance. The music for a country dance could be provided by a single fiddle, or Hardanger fiddle. At times ensembles of musicians all playing the same instrument, such as accordions, harps, or fiddles, provided the music. After 1800, runddans, or turning dances, became popular. Runddans were newer modern dances from other parts of Europe. The music for the runddans is provided by a group playing a variety of instruments rather than just one. Fiddle and accordion solos are common in the music for runddans.

Norway has a thriving musical tradition of opera, symphonies, bands, shows, and nightclubs. Among the country's many past and present musical talents are: violinists Ole Bull, Arve Tellefsen, and Henny Kraggerud; composers Edvard Grieg, Geirr Tveitt, Lasse Thoresen, and Cecilie Ore; jazz musicians Jan Garbarek and Nils-Petter Molvær; and Sami singer Mari Boine Persen.

ARCHITECTURE

Historically, the most accessible building material in Norway was wood, because of the vast Norwegian forests. While Norway was building wooden structures, other European centers were building homes, churches, and public buildings from stone and related materials. One notable Norwegian exception to wooden structures is Trondheim's Nidaros Cathedral. Building on this stone structure began almost one thousand years ago and took over 300 years to complete. It is of English Gothic design and lies over the grave of Saint Olav.

Norway is a land of diverse architectural styling. In just the last two hundred years, it has evolved from an urban environment dominated by high-density brick apartment buildings called "wolf houses" or "New York," to an urban landscape that reflects many styles of architecture. By the 1850s, new neighborhoods with spacious lots and stately homes surrounded older urban housing and industries. By the early 1900s, open environmental spaces became important settings for homes. Today, Norwegian architecture demonstrates a great interest in environmentally friendly building materials, natural settings, and healthy homes.

ART AND ARTIFACTS

Numerous museums and heritage centers are found across the Norwegian landscape. These museums and cultural centers include small preserved farmsteads, museums dedicated to single influential individuals, ship museums, forestry museums, and cultural heritage centers and parks. Among the more notable are the National Gallery, the Natural History Museum and Botanical Gardens, the Oslo Ship Museum, and the Ethnographic Museum, all in Oslo. The fine arts are recognized in museums dedicated to composer Edvard Grieg in Troldhaugen, writer Henrik Ibsen in Oslo, and singer Kirsten Flagstad in Hamar.

Art in its most traditional form is visible in the numerous examples of rose maling. Norwegians developed the art of rose maling during the eighteenth century. It consists of hand-painting decorative flowers on household furnishings and surfaces, especially in kitchens. The most commonly painted are wooden trunks, tables and chairs, and ceilings and walls.

Skilled Norwegian artisans also have gained recognition for their design of furniture, household items, and jewelry. Painting has a long history in Norway. Perhaps the most famous artist was Edvard Munch, noted for his somewhat morbid work, *The Scream*. Other noted figures include landscape artist J. C. Dahl, illustrator Theodor Kittlesen, and modernist Odd Nerdrum. Sculpture is also an important art form in Norway.

SPORTS

The Norwegian people love sports and recreation. Their interests are seasonal, with activities clearly distinguishing between winter and summer seasons. Because of the country's

Cross-country skiing is very popular in Norway where there are over 18,500 miles (29,772 kilometers) of ski trails.

geographic location and resulting climate, winter sports and recreation are especially popular. This love for winter sports was most obvious when Norway hosted the 1994 Olympic Winter Games at Lillehammer. Gold-medal-winning figure skater Sonja Henie, skier Stein Eriksen, and biathlete Ole Einar Bjoerndalen attest to the competitiveness of Norway's Winter Olympians.

Cross-country skiing and ice skating are especially popular activities in Norway. Over 18,500 miles (29,772 kilometers) of cross-country ski trails crisscross the landscape. Many of these ski trails are lit during the dark winters and at night. Outdoor ice skating rinks dot the country, providing facilities for hockey, speed skating, figure skating, and free skating. Alpine skiing and ski jumping are also popular, with hundreds of chair lifts, tows, and ski jumps available for enthusiasts. Some of the more competitive citizens enjoy Nordic combined skiing, the biathlon, bobsledding, and tobogganing.

Summer recreation and sports also center on the outdoors. Walking, jogging, hiking, and biking are popular summer activities. Water is everywhere, so fishing, swimming, and boating are enjoyed widely. Norwegians, like most Europeans, love football (soccer) and go wild when their men's and women's teams play in the World Cup. Over 1,800 different soccer teams play at all levels across the country. No matter what the season, the Norwegian people enjoy outdoor recreation and sports on a level matched by few other countries.

GENEALOGY

One of the major forces behind the increasing interest in Norwegian genealogy is coming from people of Norwegian ancestry in the United States and Canada. The U.S. Census in 2000 indicated that almost 4.5 million Americans are of Norwegian ancestry.

Because Norwegian immigration is somewhat recent, significant oral and written knowledge about one's ancestors or home area is often available, providing an important starting point to trace family history. For people seeking genealogical information, Norway offers all the traditional resources, including church records, birth and death records, probate records, and census records. A unique additional resource is the *bygdebøker*, a book based on a geographic area called a commune. The bygdebøker tells both the history of the community and ideally something about every family residing in the commune. Other valuable sources for genealogists interested in Norway are records related to farm life. These include land ownership and real estate tax records. Many Norwegian Americans find that it is relatively easy to trace one's ancestry back to the original family farm or village, often finding relatives along the way.

These children are parading in front of the Royal Palace in Oslo, during Norwegian Constitution Day.

Norway Looks to the Future

The process of learning and understanding the geography of Norway began with an analysis of the land's physical geography. Physically, Norway is a land almost completely comprised of mountains and valleys. Its spectacular fjords, waterfalls, and coastal islands are products of glaciation. Hundreds of glaciers continue to cover parts of the country. Three distinct climate zones are found. Southern and central Norway enjoy a relatively mild and moist west coast marine climate. In the north, the polar (tundra) climate dominates. In between the two is a small extension of the humid continental long-winter climate.

Once a land covered with pine trees, today the Norway spruce covers much of the south. Deciduous trees such as birch and aspen are found in the mountains and plateaus along with heather and grasses in the valleys and lowlands. Tundra vegetation of moss and lichen blanket the higher elevations of the mountains and much of the far north.

The first human occupants arrived from Central Asia between 8,000 and 10,000 years ago. They likely were the ancient ancestors of the Sami people. Stone Age, Bronze Age, and Iron Age peoples, primarily from Germanic lands south of the Scandinavian Peninsula, followed. While not extensive, evidence of these civilizations exists in Norway's cultural landscape, in features such as cairns, burial mounds, and stone pillars as well as in their artifacts displayed and protected in an extensive variety of museums.

For 300 years, beginning in the eighth century, the Vikings held sway on vast areas of Sweden, Denmark, Finland, Ireland, Britain, and Iceland. These seafaring warriors raided the lands for their treasures. Eventually they established forts, towns, and settlements and attempted to occupy the lands. They also intermarried, assimilated the conquered, and often brought the stories and profits of their adventures back to Norway. The Viking Age ended about 1100, following defeats in Ireland and England. During their reign, the Vikings were among the most powerful people in the world, and certainly the most powerful in Europe.

In the 1400s, independent Norway became part of the kingdom of Denmark and Norway, ruled by a Danish king. In the sixteenth century, Danish King Christian III decided that his lands should follow the Protestant Reformation and he imposed his Lutheran faith on the people. That faith became the Church of Norway. The impact of Christian III is still obvious because the state religion is still a major force in life of the Norwegian people.

Norwegians drafted a constitution in 1814, hoping independence would follow Denmark's defeat in the Napoleonic Wars. Sweden laid claim to Denmark the same year, yet the Storting continued to function. In 1905, in a nearly unanimous referendum, Norwegians voted to break from Sweden. This action, along with pressure from the Storting, convinced King Oscar that Norway should be independent. Norway became independent in 1905, choosing a Danish prince to become King Haakon VII. King Haakon VII led Norway through two world wars and the Great Depression. Oil exploration in the last 20 years has given the country access to enormous wealth, enabling Norway to remain independent and to rebuff two invitations to join the European Union.

Norway's population distribution closely corresponds with its physical geography and climate. The cold, tundra north is sparsely populated, mainly by Sami people. Areas of mountains and glaciers are also sparsely populated. Coastal zones, rivers flowing into fjords, plateaus, and valleys are home to most of Norway's population. The country long resisted urbanization, and the government's policies helped discourage urbanization. Although urbanization came late, it came, and today, over 70 percent of Norwegians live in urban areas.

Just as urbanization came late to Norway, so, too, did emigration to North America. Norwegian emigration took off during the 1860s, with Norwegians from rural areas migrating through New York and west to rural areas with agricultural lands available, such as Wisconsin, Minnesota, Iowa, and the Dakotas. Today, Norway is experiencing immigration, as well. Most immigrants come from European countries, but few of those apply for naturalization. Rather, the non-European populations from South Asia, East Asia, and more recently the Middle East, are the main groups who have become Norwegian citizens in recent years.

Like many other western countries that became more nationalistic during the nineteenth century, Norway embraced a dreadful policy of assimilation toward the Sami people two hundred years ago. Remarkably, the Sami and their language survived the assimilation efforts. A movement toward Sami nationalism during the twentieth century, coupled with a change in course by the Norwegian government, led to many advances for Sami culture in the post-World War II era. Today, the Sami language is again taught in schools and is in fact protected by the Norwegian Constitution. The recent convening of the Sami Assembly was a landmark event.

Norway is home to four languages: Bokmål, Nynorsk, Samnorsk, and Sami. What language do the people speak? What is the official language? Norway's answer is that Bokmål is the official language of the land. However, local municipalities have the authority to decide whether Bokmål or Nynorsk is taught in their schools.

The kingdom of Norway is a constitutional monarchy. Since

1814, the Storting has enacted legislation for Norway. The king plays a primarily ceremonial position in the Norwegian government. Rather, most of the power is in the Storting and the prime minister.

Although the Storting began to function in 1814 after establishment of the Norwegian Constitution, Norway did not gain its independence from Sweden until 1905. This recent independence, along with Norway's policy of providing social welfare programs to all Norwegians, regardless of location, helped Norwegians vote twice to stay out of the European Union.

The Norwegian government plays a vital role in Norway's economy. During the last 30 years, Norway has become a major world producer of petroleum and natural gas, extracted from North Sea and the Norwegian Sea. The government uses monies from the petroleum and natural gas industries to raise the standard of living of the people, fund social welfare programs, and develop long-term financial investments to protect Norwegian society.

For centuries, Norwegians passed sagas, folktales, and legends to younger generations through storytelling. Today, Norway is home to three Nobel Prize winners for literature, and can boast a literacy rate of nearly 100 percent. As this story of Norway's geography draws to a close, it is important to remember that Norwegian folktales tend to be grounded in reality, as opposed to the American, "and they lived happily ever after." The reality of Norway's future is found in its ancient and recent history. Norway has experienced long stretches of dominating the northern European region and long stretches of being dominated by others. Norway has experienced isolation, independence, and internationalism. These influences are evident today in Norway's reluctance to join the European Union. The country also engages regularly in peacemaking efforts on the world stage, embraces human rights for its people and people of the world, and is home to the Nobel Peace Prize.

The reality is that Norway will continue to be pulled in the contrasting directions of isolation, independence, and internationalism. Throughout its history, Norway has used its relative isolation to push for its independence and rationalize its internationalism. That is the end of this story, and it is the future of Norway.

Name	Kingdom of Norway.
Relative location	Part of the Scandinavian peninsula, bordering the North Sea, the Norwegian Sea, and the North Atlantic Ocean, west of Sweden.
Area	125,182 square miles (324,220 square kilometers).
Coastline	13,624 miles (21,925 kilometers).
Climate	Three climatic zones: marine west coast, humid continental – long winter, and polar (tundra).
Terrain	Hundreds of mountain peaks, high plateaus, fertile valleys, fjorded coastlines, and Arctic tundra in the north.
Elevations	Sea level to 8,100 feet (2,469 meters) (Mt. Galdhopiggen).
Minerals	Petroleum, natural gas, iron ore, copper, ilmenite.
Population	4,525,116 (2002).
Religions	Church of Norway 86% (state church), Roman Catholic and other Protestant religions 3%, other 1%, none and unknown 10% (1997).
Languages	Norwegian (Bokmål, Nynorsk, and Samnorsk), and Sami.
Literacy	100%.
Capital	Oslo.
Counties	19 counties: Akershus, Aust-Agder, Buskerud, Finnmark, Hedmark, Hordaland, More og Romsdal, Nordland, Nord-Trondelag, Oppland, Oslo, Ostfold, Rogaland, Sogn og Fjordane, Sor-Trondelag, Telemark, Troms, Vest-Agder, Vestfold.
Independence Day	7 June 1905, Norway declared the union with Sweden dissolved. 6 October 1905, Sweden agreed to the repeal of the union.
National holiday	Constitution Day, 17 May (1814).
Flag	Red background, with a blue cross outlined in white.
Industries	Petroleum and gas, food processing, shipbuilding, pulp and paper products, and fishing.

Exports	Petroleum and petroleum products, machinery and equipment, metals, ships, and fish.
Imports	Food stuffs, machinery and equipment, chemicals, and metals.
Currency	Norwegian Krone.
Railways	2,493 miles (4,012 kilometers) of standard gauge; 1,572 miles (2,530 kilometers) are electrified track.
Highways	42,155 miles (67,838 kilometers) paved road (includes 68 miles, or 109 kilometers of expressways). 74% of roads paved (1999).
Waterways	980 miles (1,577 kilometers) along west coast.
Major airports	Oslo, Bergen, Stavanger, Trondheim.
Major ports	Oslo, Bergen, Trondheim, Stavanger, Kristiansand.

12,000 B.C.	Ice Age ends. Landscape again visible, plant life blossoms.
8,000 B.C.	First human occupants appear on the Norwegian landscape.
5,000 B.C.	Germanic agriculturalists arrive in Norway.
1,800 B.C.	Bronze Age people arrive in Norway.
500 B.C.	Iron Age reaches Norway from Germanic south. For next 1,000 years, people live in relative isolation from the rest of the world.
793 A.D.	Viking Age begins with an attack on English monastery in Lindisfarne.
840	Vikings establish city of Dublin on island of Ireland.
861	Vikings loot Paris.
874	Harald the Fair-Haired conquers petty kings. Some of the people he defeated leave to settle Iceland.
1001	Leif Eriksson reaches Vinland (North America).
1014	Forces of Brain Boru drive Vikings from Ireland.
1028	Danish King Canute invades Norway. During occupation King Olav Haraldson is martyred becoming Saint Olav the patron Saint of Norway; Christianity arrives.
1050	Oslo founded.
1066	Viking Age ends with loss at Battle of Stamford Bridge in England.
1130	Sigrud I's death with no heir begins long period without leadership.
1217	King Haakon IV restores the power of the monarchy in Norway.
1349	The black plague kills off one-half of Norway's population.
1397	Union of Norway, Sweden, and Denmark established on Trinity Sunday.
1536	Danish noblemen take control of Norway.
1537	Danes impose Protestantism as the religion of the land. Evangelical Lutheran church becomes the state church of Norway.
1814	Defeat of Napoleon by British placed Norway under control of Sweden. On May 17, 1814, Norway adopts its constitution.
1825	Great migration to America began.
1884	Political parties are established in Norway.

1905	National referendum leads to complete independence from Sweden. The Storting invites Danish Prince Carl to become King Haakon VII of Norway.
1913	Women granted the right to vote.
1929	Worldwide Great Depression sets stage for emergence of Hitler in Germany.
1940	Norway invaded by German forces despite its neutrality.
1945	King Haakon returns from exile following the end of WWII. Norway joins the United Nations.
1949	Norway joins North Atlantic Treaty Organization.
1961	Oil discovered in the North Sea.
1972	Norway declines to join European Union.
1994	Norway again declines to join the European Union. Olympic Winter Games are held at Lillehammer.
2001	Norway elected to United Nations Security Council.

Andersen, Waltraud. *Baedeker's Scandinavia*. Englewood Cliffs, NJ: Prentice Hall, 1982.

Blashfield, Jean F. *Norway*. New York: Children's Press, 2000.

Blehr, Barbro. Sacred unity, sacred similarity: Norwegian Constitution Day parades. *Ethnology* 38 (2): 175–89, 1999.

Central Intelligence Agency. 2002. *The World Factbook 2001*. Washington, DC. *http://www.cia.gov/cia/publications/factbook/*.

Conger, Margaret M. 2001. Health and social services for the elderly: a comparative analysis. *Nursing Economics* 19 (6): 277–283.

Fullerton, Brian, and Alan F. Williams. *Scandinavia*. New York: Praeger Publishers, 1972.

Hintz, Martin. *Norway*. New York: Children's Press, 1995.

Insight Guide. *Norway*. Maspeth, New York: Langenscheidt Publishers, 2002.

Kiel, Anne Cohen, ed. *Continuity and change: Aspects of contemporary Norway*. Oxford: Scandinavian University Press, 1993.

Margeson, Susan M. *Viking*. New York: Alfred A. Knopf. 1994.

Mead, W. R. *An Historical Geography of Scandinavia*. London: Academic Press, 1981.

Ministry of Finance. *Statistics Norway*. Oslo, Norway. *http://www.ssb.no/english/*.

Ministry of Foreign Affairs. *ODIN*. Oslo, Norway. *http://odin.dep.no/odin/engelsk/index-b-n-a.html*.

Murphy, Alexander B., and Hunderi-Ely, A. 1996. The geography of the 1994 Nordic vote on European Union membership. *The Professional Geographer* 48 (3): 284–297.

Norwegian Tourist Board. *Norway Tourist Guide*. Oslo, Norway. *http://www.visitnorway.com/*.

Oxenstierna, Eric Graf. *The world of the Norsemen*. Cleveland: The World Publishing Company, 1967.

Ryvarden, Leif. *The Flora and Fauna of Norway*. ODIN. Oslo, Norway. *http://odin.dep.no/odin/engelsk/norway/environment/032005-990402/index-dok000-b-n-a.html*.

Søme, Axel. *A Geography of Norden*. London: Heinemann, 1968.

Index

Index

Index

Index

Index

page:

About the Contributors

ERIN HOGAN FOUBERG is adjunct associate professor of geography at South Dakota State University in Brookings, South Dakota. She co-edited the book *The Tribes and States: Geographies of Intergovernmental Interaction* (Roman and Littlefield, 2002). She is the author of *Tribal Territory, Sovereignty, and Governance: A Study of the Cheyenne River and Lake Traverse Indian Reservations* (Garland, 2000) and co-authored with her father *Ireland* (Chelsea House, 2003) and *The Geography of South Dakota* (Center for Western Studies, 3rd Edition, 2001). Aside from her work on jurisdiction in Indian country, Dr. Fouberg has published on the use of writing in geographic education, and has co-edited a special issue of the *Journal of Geography* on education theory in geography. The students at Mary Washington College in Fredericksburg, Virginia honored Dr. Fouberg in 2001 with the Mary Pinschmidt Award for the professor most likely to be remembered for having an impact on their lives.

EDWARD PATRICK HOGAN is professor emeritus of geography at South Dakota State University and the State Geographer of South Dakota. He and his wife Joan have made several trips to Europe over the last eight years. In addition to his career teaching geography, Ed is associate vice president for academic affairs and chief information technology officer for South Dakota State University. Ed and his daughter Erin Hogan Fouberg have co-authored *Ireland* (Chelsea House, 2003) and *The Geography of South Dakota* (Center for Western Studies, 2001). Ed has authored numerous articles, television series, and publications related to types of housing around the world, migration, economic development, and regional geography. He received the Distinguished Teaching Award from the National Council for Geographic Education and in 1992 was included in the book *Leaders in American Geography* as one of 79 people who have most influenced geographic education in the United States. He especially enjoys being with his family, listening to traditional Irish music, and creating works of art.

CHARLES F. ("FRITZ") GRITZNER is Distinguished Professor of Geography at South Dakota University in Brookings. He is now in his fifth decade of college teaching and research. During his career, he has taught more than 60 different courses, spanning the fields of physical, cultural, and regional geography. In addition to his teaching, he enjoys writing, working with teachers, and sharing his love for geography with students. As consulting editor for the MODERN WORLD NATIONS series, he has a wonderful opportunity to combine each of these "hobbies." Fritz has served as both president and executive director of the National Council for Geographic Education and has received the Council's highest honor, the George J. Miller Award for Distinguished Service.